High Heels
in the
TUNDRA

My Life as a Geographer and Climatologist

MARIE SANDERSON

iUniverse, Inc.
New York Bloomington

High Heels in the Tundra
My Life as a Geographer and Climatologist

iUniverse books may be ordered through booksellers or by contacting:

iUniverse
1663 Liberty Drive
Bloomington, IN 47403
www.iuniverse.com
1-800-Authors (1-800-288-4677)

ISBN: 978-1-4401-4720-3 (pbk)
ISBN: 978-1-4401-4721-0 (ebk)

Printed in the United States of America

iUniverse rev. date: 6/17/2009

Dedication and Acknowledgements

This book is dedicated to my family: children, grandchildren, in-laws and siblings, and to the many scientists whose names appear in these pages.

I thank my friend and former student, David Phillips, for suggesting the title. I thank the people at iUniverse for guiding me through the publishing process. My most sincere thanks are given to my geography colleague and friend, Philip Howarth, for his computer assistance and excellent advice during the long gestation period of "High Heels in the Tundra."

Contents

CHAPTER 1
The Incipient Geographer

This book is the story of my life as a pioneer Canadian geographer and climatologist. After my eightieth birthday, I decided to write about my many years of geographic and climate explorations of this fascinating world. Of course, the book also contains some stories about my personal life as a daughter, friend, wife, mother and grandmother.

I owe my existence to the fact that my grandmother was seasick. My mother's mother, Christina Marie Werner, was born in Baden Baden, Germany in 1860. When she was 16 years old, some neighbours, who were emigrating to Canada, asked her to accompany them as a mother's helper. The ocean voyage took six weeks in those days and my grandmother was violently seasick. When they finally arrived at their destination – Port Elgin on the shores of Lake Huron in Bruce County, Ontario – she decided that she could not face the return voyage to Germany. She never saw her family again. There was a German community in Port Elgin and she eventually met and married Conrad Kuhl, another German immigrant. They had three children: two boys,

George and Milton, and one daughter, Martha, my mother, who was born in1890. Conrad died quite young and my grandmother was left to raise her three children alone. My mother left school at the age of 16 to work in a tailor's shop to help support the family. The skills she learned there proved useful in her later life when making clothes for her three daughters.

My father, William Lustig, was born in Listowel, near Kitchener, Ontario in 1880. His parents had emigrated to Canada from northern Germany, near Hannover, where his father had served in the Prussian army. Like my maternal grandfather, my father's father died at a young age, leaving eight children. At the age of 20, my father (Will as he was always called) moved to Chesley in Bruce County, about 30 km south of Owen Sound, to start a butcher business. He was attracted to the town because a German furniture-making family, the Krugs, had moved their business from Kitchener to Chesley. It was then a town of about 1,700 people, with a mixed Scottish-German population.

My father also entered into a partnership with two other men to build a skating rink, successfully obtaining a bank loan of $2,000, a large sum in those days, to construct the rink. All his life my father was keen about skating and hockey, often recruiting hockey players for the Chesley Colts by obtaining jobs for them in the furniture factory. Later, he also became interested in figure skating, after Sonja Heine's great success at the sport, and started a figure skating club in Chesley. My mother was also quite a sports enthusiast. She loved skating and snowshoeing, and before she was married, would often snowshoe to Southampton, 10 km away, and return to Port Elgin by train. She never learned to swim, although she spent a good deal of her childhood at Port Elgin's beautiful beach. At that time, it was not considered proper for girls to swim.

Through their mutual interest in skating, my parents met, fell in love and were married in 1917. My mother was 27 years old, quite an advanced age for marriage in those days, and my father was 37. He had delayed marriage since he was the main support of his family after the death of his father. At first the couple lived with my father's mother, until my mother insisted on a home of their own. My father bought a lovely property of about 20 acres at the edge of town, bordering the Saugeen River. Five children were born: Harry, Marie, Gwen, George, and Joan. In a small town like Chesley, where very few young people went to university, our family was unusual in having four children with university degrees. All three daughters are graduates in geography from the University of Toronto.

I had a very happy childhood. Since our house was close to the Saugeen River, we swam there in the summer, and if there wasn't too much snow, skated there in winter. There was a nice hill for tobogganing and sleigh riding. Since our father owned the skating rink, I spent a lot of time there. I loved skating. I remember that the rink had a wonderful Wurlitzer organ that played waltzes. When my sister Gwen and I were in our teens, our father arranged for us to take figure skating lessons in Owen Sound. He was certainly ahead of his time in seeing the future popularity of figure skating.

The 1930s were usually known as the depression years in Canada, but I don't remember that our family suffered any hardships. Our meat came from our father's shop and we had a large vegetable garden. There was no electric refrigeration in those days, but people had iceboxes which had to be supplied with large blocks of ice each week. The ice business was another of my father's interests. In the late winter, his employees would cut large blocks of ice from the river and store them in an "ice house" behind our house. To slow the melting, layers of sawdust were placed between the layers of ice. What a fantastic place to play on hot summer days!

During those years of depression I remember that "tramps" (as my mother called them) would come to our house to ask for food, and she always fed them a good meal on our back porch. I especially remember the year 1936. The heat wave that summer was the worst weather disaster of a non-maritime nature in Canadian history, killing 780 people. My personal recollection of that year was that my father slept on the front verandah, an unheard-of activity for him. I also remember infestations of tent caterpillars that derailed trains, and fell from the trees. I was terrified that one would fall on my head, so I walked to school in the middle of the road. Boys would put them in our desks at school. I have always since had a hatred of caterpillars.

Books were very important in our family. My father used to read to us in the evenings, usually Thornton Burgess animal stories about Reddy Fox and Sammy Jay and Farmer Brown, wonderful stories for children. My mother was an avid reader, who introduced me to the local library as soon as I could read. I went every week to borrow the maximum number of books allowed. I remember thinking that perhaps I could read all the books in the library. My very first memory, when I was probably four or five years old, was playing school with my friends. I was always the teacher. I loved the day I finally went to school. I was a competitive student and always wanted to be first in my class. In my graduation year from public school, there was a prize for the top student in Bruce County. I was devastated when the results were announced and my friend Mary won the prize, and I had come second.

I recall another incident from that year in Grade 8. I was a very talkative student and was often reprimanded by my teachers. The Grade 8 teacher was the school principal, H.S. Sanderson, a strict disciplinarian who didn't hesitate to administer "the strap" to erring students. One day I was whispering to a friend and the principal asked me to leave the room. I was terrified, certain that I would receive the strap. However, Mr. Sanderson said to me "You are a good student and probably don't need to pay attention all the time, but you are preventing others from paying attention." I didn't receive the threatened punishment, and I have always remembered that advice.

The high school in Chesley was in the same building as the public school. It was on the second floor, and I thought that was why it was called the "high" school. Geography was not on the curriculum, but high school did give me a curiosity about the natural world. I remember our botany teacher saying, "Always have a curiosity about the world around you." Another of his quotes I have remembered is the one from Tennyson:

> *I am a part of all that I have met;*
> *Yet all experience is an arch wherethro'*
> *Gleams that untravell'd world, whose margin fades*
> *Forever and forever when I move.*

That quote certainly influenced me in choosing to study geography. I wanted to learn all about the world, and I wanted to see as much of it as possible. It was like wanting to read all the books in the library.

In high school, my only "boy friend" was the principal's son, Robert Miles (Bob) Sanderson. He was tall and good-looking and a star of the football team and the Chesley Colt's hockey team. We lived quite near each other, and usually walked to school together. I remember our first "date." Since there was no movie theatre in Chesley, Bob took me (in his father's car) to the theatre in Hanover, ten miles away. I recall that the movie was *Gone With the Wind*. What a standard for future films!

Although world events seemed far removed from my life in Chesley, I do remember the outbreak of World War II in the summer of 1939. My memory is combined with the memory of the Dionne quintuplets. My father and mother, like countless others, were fascinated by the news of the birth of five little girls in Callendar in northern Ontario, and decided to drive there with our whole family to see these amazing children. Thus it was in North Bay that we heard the news of the outbreak of the Second World War. In Chesley, the war seemed very far away and didn't affect my life as a high school student, although some young men in the town eagerly enlisted in the Canadian Army or Air Force.

I graduated from high school in 1940. Although no one in my father's or mother's family had gone to university, I persuaded my parents that I should go to the University of Toronto, since my friend Mary was going there. My father suggested that I live with his sister at 601 Palmerston Avenue, near Bloor and Bathurst, so I could save money by walking to the university, but my mother disagreed and said that I would live in residence. At that time, UofT had about 8,000 students in a college system: Trinity College was Anglican, Knox was Presbyterian, St. Michael's was Catholic, Victoria was United Church, and University College was non-denominational. Since my family belonged to the United Brethren Evangelical Church, they chose non-denominational University College for me, and enrolled me at Whitney Hall, the University College women's residence on St. George Street. There were three houses in Whitney Hall – Falconer, Mulock and Cody – built around a quadrangle as British colleges were. I was lucky to be given a private room in Mulock House. I think the cost of residence was $450 per year, and the cost of tuition was $75 per year. The dean, Marion Ferguson, insisted on ladylike behaviour for her girls; no jeans or trousers, and proper manners in the dining room. Dinners were quite formal with maid service, and afterwards coffee was served from a silver service in the lounge. Curfew was at 10:30 at night, with, I think, one

1:30 a.m. leave per week. I enjoyed living in residence, and did so for my four years at Toronto.

Although the Second World War had begun, there were still many males on campus my first two years at Toronto, and formal dances and football games still occurred. I loved the formal dances, usually at the Royal York Hotel or Eaton's Round Room in the College Street store. I remember asking my mother, who made most of my clothes, to make me an evening coat of white wool with red satin lining. I loved that coat, although by my fourth year there were no more occasions on which to wear it.

Meanwhile, Bob had enrolled at the University of Western Ontario where he hoped to study medicine, because his uncle was a medical doctor in Windsor. We saw each other infrequently, usually on holidays in Chesley, and I think that I was not surprised when he told me in 1943 that, like most males his age, he had enlisted in the Armed Forces, in Bob's case, as a private in the Canadian Army.

That first year at UofT, I had little idea about what university course to take, so I decided to enroll in a general course called Social and Philosophical Studies, or "Sock and Fill" as we called it. It was a course for students wishing to take the honours (four-year) programs in Philosophy, Political Science, Economics or Geography. There were many options. I chose courses in History, Geography, Geology, Anthropology, French, English and Religious Knowledge. The last three courses were held in University College, that historic building very near Whitney Hall, while the others were university-wide courses held in different parts of the campus. There was a ten minute interval between lectures. This often meant a fast run for me, from the geography lectures in the old McMaster building (now the Faculty of Music) on Bloor Street to the Geology building on College Street.

I loved university life. When I went home for Thanksgiving, I could not stop talking about what I was learning in my lectures. I think that my parents were a little shocked when I told them of the theory of evolution, and said that my anthropology professor did not believe God created the world in seven days. I remember that anthropology course for another reason. We were required to write an essay on the theory of evolution. My grade was a D -, and the professor's comment was "glimmerings of intelligence for a bare pass."

My favourite course was the geography course taught by Griffith Taylor in the large auditorium in the McMaster building. Taylor was an impressive lecturer. Like all professors in those days, he wore a black academic gown as he paced up and down the lecture hall, darkened so he could show his slides. He was famous for those slides, four-by-four inch glass slides, with the data drawn in ink in some sort of resin, and usually containing far too much information for the student to absorb, much less copy. The text he used was his own book *Environment, Race and Migration*, which had been published by the UofT Press in 1937. He talked about the discipline of geography and its correlative nature, linking the physical to the human sciences. (Like most young people at the time, I had thought that geography was about countries and capitals.) He spoke of the war in Europe and the theories of race. I suppose that today his lectures would be called "environmental determinism," but in 1940 we students found them intensely stimulating.

A Saturday morning laboratory class was required, taught by Mildred Brookstone. The laboratory exercises were contained in a booklet called "The Geography Laboratory" written by Taylor and his sister Dorothy and published in Australia when Taylor had been a professor at the University of Sydney. Miss Brookstone was a UofT physics graduate who had just obtained the second MA degree in geography granted by that university. The first MA had been obtained by Andy Clark in 1938. From Miss Brookstone we learned about quantitative geography long before it became popular in geography curricula. The exercise I remember best was called "Pace and Compass Survey" which we carried out on the campus behind the McMaster building. The purpose was to show students that a quite accurate survey of an area could be done using only a compass and the length of the observer's pace.

At Whitney Hall it was customary to invite a professor to a monthly formal dinner. Miss Ferguson had announced that she "liked her girls to have intercourse with the professors." (We Whitney Hall "girls" found this hilarious, of course, and still talk of it today!) I suggested that Dr. Taylor be invited. I thought that my friends in Mulock House would enjoy hearing about his experiences as a member of the 1910-1912 Antarctic Expedition led by Captain Robert Falcon Scott. My generation was very familiar with the tragic story of Scott reaching the South Pole, only to find that the Norwegian explorer Amundsen had been there a month previously, and that Scott and his companions died on their way back to the base camp. Taylor was a great success at the dinner. He told stories very well, and my friends enjoyed his Australian accent, saying "Australiar" for Australia and "Canader" for Canada.

In the 1940s there were no semester-length courses, so the final exams covered the whole year's work. I studied hard for those exams, for I wanted to do well for my parents' sake. The exam results were published in the *Toronto Star,* and I recall my mother waking me one June morning saying "You came 1:4 (fourth in first-class honours)." Of course I was pleased, and looked forward to retuning to UofT, and registering in the Honours Geography course.

Griffith Taylor had persuaded the University Senate in1940 that a four-year Honours Geography program was necessary, and two students, Jim Hamilton and Mary Parker, were enrolled in that first class. Thus I was in the second class in Honours Geography with two classmates, Don Kirk and Arn Boggs. Dick Ruggles was the only student in the year behind us, so he took classes with us. The four of us had a very happy three years. I should mention here that after graduation, Don did graduate work at the University of Illinois, and tragically was killed in an airline crash in the Canadian Arctic in 1951. Arn Boggs became a high school teacher in Kitchener. I never saw either of them after graduation. Dick became a geography professor and inaugurated the Geography program at Queen's University, so I saw him quite often after graduation.

Eight courses were required that first year of the Honours program; four in Geography and four options to be chosen from the science or arts faculties. Mathematical Geography was taught by Miss Brookstone, Urban Geography and Climatology by Taylor, and The History of Geographical Thought by George Tatham, a Welsh geographer who had joined the department in 1938. I found that I preferred the geography courses that dealt with numbers - such as Mathematical Geography and Climatology. I also enjoyed Tatham's lectures, which instilled in me an interest in the history of geographical thought, an interest that I have maintained my whole life.

The four options I chose were Geology, Physics, Economics and History. I especially remember the Physics course with Dr. Satterley, who was famous for his showmanship lectures; for example, freezing goldfish in dry ice and flinging them around the classroom. I remember Harold Innis' lectures on the Economic History of Canada for a different reason. Innis was very interested in geography and had taught a geography course at Toronto before Taylor arrived. It was Innis who was largely responsible for Taylor's appointment in 1935, and they became good friends. The departments of Economics and Geography were both housed in the McMaster building on Bloor Street. However, unlike Taylor, Innis was not a good lecturer. He sat at his desk at the front of the lecture hall and read his notes. What he had to say was terrific stuff if you paid attention, but very few of the (mostly male) students paid attention, and this annoyed me. One day during his lecture, I turned around (I usually sat near the front) and said to the male students behind me, "Why don't you shut up?" At that moment, Dr. Innis raised his eyes from his notes, and looking right at me said, "Would you please leave the room?" It was a most humiliating experience. I apologized to Dr. Innis later and he replied, "Think nothing of it. You were the first person whose eye I happened to catch." What a memory of the great Harold Innis!

The fourth member of the geography staff in those days was Donald Putnam, an agricultural scientist who had been hired by Taylor in 1937. Putnam lectured on Agricultural Geography and Africa. He was not a good lecturer and we students did not appreciate his considerable talents. There is a story (true I believe) that he actually fell asleep while giving a lecture! Putnam later conducted the field trips for the department. I think that this was the part of his job that he liked best. He loved being in the field and explaining the landforms of southern Ontario to his students. He had been working for many years on the identification of the landforms with his friend Lyman Chapman of the Ontario Research Foundation. I liked Dr. Putnam, and he played a large role in my career, as these pages will show.

In our third year, Kirk, Boggs and I were hired as "demonstrators" in the first-year geography labs. This meant that we helped Miss Brookstone, and marked the assignments. I still have my letter of appointment for the year 1942-1943, signed by the bursar of the University, C.E. Higginbottom. It stated that the Board of Governors (no less) appointed me as a part-time assistant in the Department of Geography for an annual salary of $100, a considerable sum in those days. I very much enjoyed the job, especially the outdoor surveying lab which took place along Philosopher's Walk behind the Geography building. I very well remember two of my students from that year: Bill Wonders, who later founded the Department of Geography at the University of Alberta, and Don Harron, who became famous on television as "Charlie Farquharson," and a well-known actor. He used his geographical knowledge when he wrote the very amusing book entitled *The Jogfree of Canada*. In the last year of the geography program, 12 hours of geography courses and 12 hours of outside courses, plus reading courses in French and German, were required. I had quite a good knowledge of French from high school, and I had taken one year of German, so I managed to pass both language exams. An honours thesis, involving original research, was also a requirement. Most of the BA theses at that time were regional studies of parts of Ontario, and mine was no exception. I did a regional study of two townships in Bruce County, near Chesley. I enjoyed doing the research in the summer before my final year, talking to the farmers in the area, and drawing maps of land use, my first attempt at original research!

Since the number of geography students in the 1940s was small, we undergraduates were fortunate in getting to know the graduate students who came to study with Taylor. Nadine (Hooper) Deacon received her MA in 1942 and got a job at the Toronto City Planning Board. Don Kerr, who came from British Columbia for his Master's degree, later joined the department as a professor, and became my life-long friend. Chun-fen Lee from Shanghai had won a Boxer scholarship to study at Oxford in 1940, but because of the war, came to Toronto. He received his PhD degree in 1943, the first PhD degree in Geography to be awarded in Canada. Chun-fen returned to China after graduation, and became a famous geography professor at the East China Normal University in Shanghai.

We had lots of social occasions in the Department. The Taylors were very hospitable, inviting staff and students to their home in Forest Hill Village, then as now a very posh address. As senior students, we became more familiar with Taylor's history. He had spent his early years in Sydney, Australia. He studied science at the University of Sydney, and met the man who played an important role in his career, Professor (later Sir) Edgeworth David. It was David's lectures in physiography that inspired Taylor, illustrating the intimate connection between human affairs, climate and geology. Taylor told us that he had learned from David the key to successful lecturing. "How many famous scientists have I known who failed in two major aspects. They could not remember the low intelligence of the audience, and they WOULD mumble."

Taylor won a scholarship to the University of Cambridge in England, and was a student there in 1909 when Captain Scott was organizing his second Antarctic Expedition. Since the North Pole had been claimed by the Americans Peary and Cook, the Royal Geographical Society under Sir Clements Markham insisted that the South Pole be discovered by an Englishman. The British Antarctic Expedition of 1910-1912 was a serious scientific expedition, as well as an attempt to be the first at the Pole. Hundreds of applications for places on the Expedition were received by Scott, Taylor's among them. To impress Scott, Grif (as he was always called) and his friend, Canadian physicist Charles Wright, walked from Cambridge to London, a 50-mile hike, in one day. Both were invited by Scott to be members of the scientific team, Taylor as chief geologist, and Wright as physicist. Two other Cambridge friends of Grif's were also selected for the scientific team: Frank Debenham, later to become the director of the Scott Polar Research Institute in Cambridge, and Raymond (later Sir Raymond) Priestley, who would later become Grif's brother-in-law. The Antarctic Expedition was the experience of his lifetime for Taylor.

In the Antarctic, Taylor became familiar with Scott during the long months of winter darkness spent at Hut Point before the attempt on the Pole. Scott organized a series of lectures, and Grif lectured on his favourite subject, physiography. Scott was most impressed. He wrote in his detailed account of the expedition, "Taylor's intellect is omnivorous and versatile. His mind is unceasingly active, his grasp wide." Taylor was chosen by Scott to be the leader of a four-month geological exploration of the coast of Victoria Land in October, 1911, and he carried out the task extremely well. His maps of the area, accomplished using only a theodolite and pace and compass surveys, were found to be so accurate that they were not surpassed until the age of aerial photography. Many books have been written about the Expedition; the most moving was the one written by Scott himself, and published after his death. Who can forget the tragic story of Scott, Wilson, Bowers, Oates and Evans hauling their sledges 500 miles to the Pole only to find that the Norwegian Amundsen had been there a month previously. Scott's words, penned at the Pole, are unforgettable: "Great God! this is an awful place, and trouble enough to have laboured to it, without the reward of priority." And after that came the tragic attempt to return to base camp, Evans' and Oates' deaths, and finally the deaths of Scott, Wilson and Bowers just a few miles short of One Ton Depot.

After his Antarctic experience, Grif returned to Cambridge to write his geological reports of the expedition. He also wrote a book he entitled *With Scott: the Silver Lining*, a very readable account of his personal experiences in the Antarctic. He found the time to become married to his friend Raymond Priestley's sister, Doris. Taylor returned to Australia with Doris in 1914. He founded the Department of Geography at the University of Sydney, the first department of geography in Australia. His lectures and articles on the Australian environment clearly illustrated the arid nature of the interior of Australia, but they sparked negative articles in the Australian press, since the government of the day was actively encouraging settlement in the interior. The result was that Taylor's books were banned, and the Prime Minister of Australia called Taylor's statements "infamous lies." Because of this, and also perhaps because he was wishing to move, Taylor accepted a position in the prestigious Department of Geography at the University of Chicago in 1928. He remained there for seven years.

The story of how Taylor came to Toronto owes much to Harold Innis. In 1929, he invited Taylor to speak to the Royal Canadian Institute in Toronto. It was his first visit to Canada, and he liked the fact that Canada was part of the British Commonwealth. Innis was impressed with Taylor, and he also had the ear of University of Toronto's President Falconer. In 1931, Innis wrote to Taylor, asking him if he would consider coming to Toronto to inaugurate a Department of Geography. "Your appointment would solve all problems, giving us a strong department to start out. Geography would be enormously advanced in Canada." Taylor replied that he would be very interested in the position. However, the 1930s were depression years in Canada and Taylor heard nothing for several years. Finally, in 1935, Falconer retired and the new president, Canon Cody, invited Taylor to inaugurate the first department of geography in Canada at the University of Toronto. The inauguration ceremony, attended by university officials, the Lieutenant-Governor of Ontario and a thousand guests, was reported in *The Globe and Mail*.

At Toronto, Taylor's status as an Australian geographer in North America changed to one of the most eminent geographers of his time. In 1941, he was elected President of the Association of American Geographers, one of the few non-Americans to have been so honoured. He also found time to write and travel in spite of his heavy teaching schedule. *Environment, Race and Migration* was published in 1937, *Our Evolving Civilization* in 1946, *Urban Geography* in1949, and *Geography in the Twentieth Century* in 1951. He saw most of Canada before writing his regional geography text *Canada*, travelling by train across the continent, and by steamer down the Mackenzie River as far as Tuktoyaktuk. In all, he published 20 books and 200 articles on his beloved geography! As Taylor's students, we knew that we were fortunate in studying with such a distinguished geographer. But also, behind his gruff exterior, he was a kind and considerate man. He kept in touch with his students, and worked hard to obtain jobs and scholarships for them. Certainly I was a recipient of his concern, as these pages will show.

I graduated in June, 1944. My mother made me a white graduation dress, and she and my father came to the graduation, and met Dr. Taylor. I carried red roses in the procession to Convocation Hall. I knelt in front of the Chancellor, Sir William Mulock, to receive my degree, and with my family, had a celebration luncheon at the Park Plaza Hotel. It was a wonderful day! But I did feel sad to be leaving UofT. I had loved university life and my geography courses. I had met Dr. Taylor, and decided that I would be a geographer. However, I felt that it was time to earn a living.

I asked Dr. Taylor for advice, and he suggested that I apply for a job with Dr. Eugene Faludi, a city planner from Italy who had been hired by the City of Toronto to make plans for post-war Toronto. Probably because of Taylor's recommendation, I was hired as an assistant planner by Dr. Faludi, and in the fall of 1944 began to work with him at the city planning offices in the Toronto Art Gallery, now the Art Gallery of Ontario. My job was to help with displays of Faludi's plans for post-war Toronto. One task I remember vividly was making a plywood model of the city, using a jigsaw in the Department of Engineering at UofT. It's amazing that I didn't cut off any fingers!

After several months, I decided that there wasn't much future for me in the city planning job. Just at that time Dr. Taylor contacted me to say that he had received a letter from an American geographer friend, O.E.Baker, who had recently inaugurated a Department of Geography at the University of Maryland. Dr. Taylor wondered if I would be interested in applying for a graduate scholarship in the new department in Maryland. I was certainly interested. I had no idea where Maryland was, but I was eager to return to university. I told my parents about the scholarship, and they agreed that I should apply. Such modern parents who believed that a daughter should not only have a BA degree, but should go to graduate school! I knew that the timing was right for a female applicant, since the United States was engaged in World War II, and few male students would apply. My application was quickly accepted. I couldn't believe my good fortune; that I would be a graduate student in geography, and in a foreign country.

CHAPTER 2
A Student of Climate

In January, 1945, I left Toronto by train for my first trip outside Ontario, to begin my studies at the University of Maryland, located in College Park, a suburb of Washington. It was an overnight trip (sitting up, of course), and it seemed exotic to me to see in the morning a different-looking foreign country. I was met at the Washington station by Dr. Baker's secretary, and we went by bus to Dr. Baker's house, located on the campus of the university. How different the campus looked from that at UofT – all red brick and white pillars. To my eyes it looked very southern, as in the movie *Gone with the Wind*. Dr. Baker and his family were unbelievably friendly, and insisted that I stay with them until I found a place to live. They were Quakers, the first I had ever met, and I was surprised that they lived such a simple and rural life in the suburbs of the country's capital.

My first priority was finding a place to live. I was very pleased when Dr. Baker arranged for me to live in the Pi Phi sorority house at no cost, in exchange for helping in the dining room. It was not a difficult job, and the Pi Phi girls were very friendly to the foreigner in their house. I did feel like a foreigner when they asked me if the University of Toronto was "in McGill," or when they teased me that Canada had no Fourth of July, that our calendar went from July the third to July the fifth! My roommate was Nancy from Oregon, a graduate student in English.

It was an exciting experience to live only a half hour from Washington, a beautiful city. I lost no time in exploring the monuments – the Capitol, the Lincoln and Jefferson memorials – and I climbed to the top of the Washington Monument. That winter was unusually cold for Washington, and the reflecting pond between the two memorials became frozen for a short period of time. I had brought my skates from Canada and went skating on the pond. I don't think many people have done that! The city was unbelievably lovely in the spring when the cherry blossoms were out. I explored the many museums and art galleries, and was especially thrilled when Dr. Baker arranged for me to have a pass to use the Library of Congress.

I enrolled in Dr. Baker's Agricultural Geography course, and a Physical Geography course taught by Dr. van Royen, a Dutch geographer who was the only other professor in the department. When I told my professors that my degree was in Honours Geography (meaning a four-year program), I was told that the University of Maryland did not believe in the honours system. Early in the term, Dr. Baker discussed with me a possible topic for my Master's thesis. Because of his interest in agriculture, he suggested the topic "Limits of Crops in Western Canada" and as early as January, 1945, he wrote to Griffith Taylor about my thesis and gave me a copy of the letter:

> *Many thanks for your note of January 15. Miss Lustig has arrived and is now down in the city with Dr. van Royen working in one of the large libraries. It occurred to me that, in view of Miss Lustig's familiarity with Canadian conditions and sources of data, she might make her thesis relate to the climate and soil correlations of the major Canadian crops.*

It was a long letter, outlining the many topics that Dr. Baker thought I should include in my thesis. I was a little worried about his phrase "familiarity with Canadian conditions," since I had never seen anything of Canada outside southern Ontario, had taken only one course in Canadian geography, and knew nothing of the climate and soil conditions of the major Canadian crops. However, I felt that I would learn much from Dr. Baker and his agricultural courses.

I began to realize what a renowned scientist Dr. Baker was – a world-class agricultural geographer and population expert. Born in 1883, he had earned degrees in history and philosophy from Heidelberg College in Ohio, and Columbia University in New York, and a PhD degree in economics from the University of Wisconsin. He had worked at the U.S. Department of Agriculture in Washington from 1912 until 1938. His *Atlas of World Agriculture* with Vernon Finch in 1915, and his *Atlas of American Agriculture* in 1936 earned him an international reputation. In a switch in careers in 1942, he accepted an invitation from the University of Maryland to establish a department of geography, although he had no training in academic geography.

I was a little lonely that spring and felt a long way from home. I kept in touch with my family in Canada and Bob in Europe by letter (phone calls were for emergencies only). On March 1, I received a letter from my mother telling me that Bob, who was then with the Essex Scottish Regiment of the Canadian Army in Europe, was reported "missing in action" on February 19th. Of course I knew that in war, soldiers were killed or wounded or taken prisoner, but I never thought that it could happen to "my" soldier. I continued to send letters to Bob, but didn't know for three months if he were alive or dead.

Finally on May 1, I received a letter from Bob from a hospital in England. He wrote that on that fateful day in February, his unit had been overrun by a German Panzer Division near Cleve in Germany. He had been taken prisoner while attempting to look after his friend who had been wounded by a grenade. He wrote that he would always be grateful to the German soldier who did not shoot him, but took him and his friend as prisoners-of-war. (For the rest of his life, Bob celebrated February 19th as his second birthday.) With about one hundred other prisoners, he was taken by cattle car to Stalag 11B, a prisoner-of-war camp near Hannover in Germany. He wrote that at the camp, which was very crowded with prisoners of every nationality, he hadn't been maltreated, but food was scarce and many prisoners died. He wrote that it was a terrible feeling to be hungry all the time, and that he had lost 50 pounds from his six-foot frame. The camp had been liberated by British troops in May, and Bob was flown to a hospital in England where he was finally able to write letters to say that he was still alive. To know that Bob had survived the war was wonderful news, but I did not see him until he was repatriated to Canada in the spring of 1946.

My life in College Park continued to be busy and interesting. I liked my lectures, and I liked living with the girls in the Pi Phi sorority house. I don't remember that I had any dates, or men friends. There were very few men on campus. I spent quite a bit of time in Washington in the Library of Congress, or visiting the many art galleries. I remember vividly the celebrations in Washington for the end of the war in Europe in the spring of 1945. Another event that I remember was the funeral of President Roosevelt. I stood with the crowds near the White House as the cortege passed, and I was moved by the silence and the obvious grief of the people around me.

During the Easter vacation, Nancy and I went on a bicycle trip to the Eastern Shore of Maryland. We biked to Annapolis, and then took the ferry (there was no bridge then) across Chesapeake Bay to the Eastern Shore. I recall being surprised at the rural nature of the Shore and how friendly the people were. We ended our trip at Rehoboth on the Atlantic coast where we sun bathed and even swam in the cold ocean. It was lucky for us that the terrain was quite flat, since we were not very competent cyclists. I think that the trip was about 200 miles; certainly the longest bicycle ride I have ever done.

In June, the term ended and I returned to Canada. Again Dr. Taylor had been busy on my behalf, and I was hired as a counsellor at Camp Tanamakoon, a girls' camp in Algonquin Park. My job was to teach the girls about maps and map reading. I remember that I went by train to Cache Lake Landing, where the old Algonquin Hotel was located, and then by canoe to Tanamakoon on Lake Tanamakoon. It was, and still is, a beautiful spot. I'm not sure how much geography I taught the campers, but I recall taking the older campers into the woods with maps and compass, and we never got lost. Mary Hamilton (we always called her Miss Hamilton) was the camp director, and she certainly instilled in her campers, and me, a love of the Canadian Shield and Algonquin Park. I think that I will always remember morning flag-raising with the campers reciting "Salutation to the Dawn," and evening campfires as we sang "Blue lake and rocky shore, I will return once more." Although we seemed very remote from world affairs, we did hear in August the great news of the end of the war. I think we celebrated by paddling over to the Algonquin Hotel for a dance. It was a perfect summer job, and an idyllic two months before returning to my life as a graduate student.

I returned to College Park in September, 1945, to a very different campus. Veterans were returning to university in large numbers, and I was asked to teach the first-year laboratory classes to mostly male students older than I was. I was also hired as a "house mother" in a university residence, a great job since it involved very little work in exchange for room and board. I began research on my thesis, searching the library for reports on the soils and crop production in the Canadian northwest.

Dr. Baker suggested that I take a course in climatology with Dr. Thornthwaite, who worked at the time in the U.S. Department of Agriculture in Washington, so would give the course in the evening in College Park. I had heard the name Thornthwaite from Dr. Taylor, whose course in climatology I had taken at UofT. Taylor had explained that climatologists in those days were very interested in classifying climates, following the example of the biologists in classifying plants. He taught us the climate classification of the famous German scientist Vladimir Köppen, which had been published in English in the 1920s. Köppen was a brilliant and innovative atmospheric scientist. He was familiar with the world distribution of plant types, and realized that climate played the major role in their distribution. He also had access to the world maps of temperature and precipitation published by the German meteorologist H.W. Dove in the late 1800s.

I must explain that thermometers to measure air temperature were not invented until the late 18th century. Also, there had been little agreement among scientists about the height at which air temperature should be measured. This problem was not solved until 1850 when the English civil engineer, Thomas Stevenson, invented the Stevenson screen, in which the thermometers were sheltered from direct sunlight, and were mounted at a height of 1.5 metres above a grass-covered surface. Amazingly this method of taking air temperature was adopted by scientists world-wide (as it still is today), and data on air temperature from different countries became comparable. Dove was thus able to construct the first world maps of temperature.

For his climate classification, Köppen used the current world maps of plant distribution and Dove's maps to identify isolines of temperature that most closely agreed with the plant boundaries. He gave letters to the various climate types: "A" for the tropical rain forest, to "E" for a frost climate. The moisture factor was identified by a second letter; for example, "s" meant summer dry. Köppen spent his lifetime refining his climate classification, and it gained world-wide recognition. One of its chief advantages was that the climate types could be shown on a single map.

In his lectures at UofT, Taylor had also mentioned another classification of climate by the American geographer C.W. Thornthwaite, published in 1931 with the title *The Climates of North America According to a New Classification*. Taylor mentioned that this classification was based not on plant distribution, but the relationship between real climatic variables: the precipitation on the earth's surface, and the evaporation from that surface. It was a mathematical and cumbersome classification, and we students (and I think Taylor himself) did not think highly of it. However, as a graduate student, I was impressed that I would be taking a course from this distinguished climatologist, and I looked forward to his lectures.

Dr. Thornthwaite was an inspiring lecturer, disliking formal presentation and preferring a mentor-student relationship. There were only three students in the class, so lectures were quite informal. We found out a little about Dr. Thornthwaite's background. He was born in 1899 in a small town in central Michigan. He had taught school in Michigan before going to California to study with Carl Sauer, a very distinguished geographer at the University of California at Berkeley. He had obtained his PhD with Sauer, and had taught geography at the University of Oklahoma, before coming to Washington in 1934 to work with the Soil Conservation Service of the U.S. Department of Agriculture. It was at the SCS that he became interested in actual research in micrometeorology, the use of water by plants, and the design of meteorological instruments. In the 1940s, he also began working on a new classification of climates, in which the central concept was potential evapotranspiration, a new term in climatology that he explained to us.

Dr. Thornthwaite pointed out that there are two aspects of evapotranspiration (the loss of water from the earth's surface). Actual evapotranspiration is the amount of water leaving the surface under variable soil moisture conditions, while potential evapotranspiration (PE) is the amount of water that would be lost if an unlimited supply of soil moisture exists. He stated that the amount of water leaving the earth's surface differs from that received by precipitation, and is more difficult to measure. Precipitation is collected in rain gauges and the amounts are recorded at climate stations around the world, while evapotranspiration must be studied by biological methods, which at that time were unfamiliar to the meteorologist or climatologist. To estimate the amount of PE from the surface of the United States, Dr. Thornthwaite used the data he had gathered on the use of water by irrigated crops in different parts of the country. He developed a formula to compute monthly amounts of potential evapotranspiration for a place using only its latitude and temperature. He explained his "water budget" technique, a month-by-month accounting of water inputs into, and withdrawals from, the earth's surface. This water budget makes it possible to quantify the hydroclimatic factors of water surplus, water deficit, soil moisture storage and actual evapotranspiration for any place with temperature and precipitation records. As his students, we were excited to be involved in the development of Dr. Thornthwaite's ideas of potential evapotranspiration and the water budget, which would not be published until 1948 as "Toward a Rational Classification of Climate."

With regard to his interest in climate classification, he explained to us that the Köppen classification, formulated for Europe, did not correctly describe the North American climates, and that his (Thornthwaite's) water budget technique could lead to a new and rational climate classification of the United States. Unlike Köppen, who stressed the temperature factor in climate, Thornthwaite recognized the importance of the moisture factor. He identified six moisture types in the United States, from perhumid (very moist) to humid, moist subhumid, dry subhumid, semiarid and arid. He used letters (A for perhumid to E for arid) to identify the various moisture regions. He identified potential evapotranspiration as the important heat factor. Again he used letters (A' to E') to identify the temperature classes: A' for the hottest or megathermal climates to E' for the frost climates. He admitted that, unlike the Köppen classification, his new classification of climate could not be shown on a single map.

I came home for Christmas full of enthusiasm for my new interest, climatology, and returned to College Park determined to write my Master's thesis with an emphasis on the climatic factors limiting crop production in the Canadian Northwest. I began researching the climate records of the Northwest Territories (NWT) and found that almost all the stations were located along the Mackenzie River, usually at the original forts founded by the fur traders, Fort Smith, Fort Simpson, Fort Norman and Fort Good Hope. I applied the water-budget technique to determine the need of the crops for water (PE) to compare with the supply (precipitation). At Fort Norman, just below the Arctic Circle, I found that the annual water need was 16.6 inches, while the annual precipitation was only 11.2 inches, resulting in an annual deficiency of 5.4 inches. (In the 1940s, Canada had not converted to the Metric system.) I was surprised to find that for all the NWT climate stations, need surpassed supply in an average year, resulting in water deficiency and a subhumid climate. This was in direct contrast to the popular notion of small water need and a humid climate in the NWT. There certainly were trees, which didn't seem to fit the idea of a subhumid climate. When I discussed this with Dr. Baker, he suggested that I contact Hugh Raup at Harvard University's Arnold Arboretum, an expert on crops and drought. I wrote to Dr. Raup and told him of my findings and he was kind enough to reply:

> *I have some pictures and notes made in the southern Yukon and northern British Columbia in the summers of 1944 and 1945, but I am hesitant to say that they represent "drought." The relation between vegetation and existing climate in that region is not necessarily a close one. It is affected by the presence of permanently frozen ground which dates from the Pleistocene. I think that if temperature and atmospheric moisture were looked upon as controlling influences, most of northwestern Canada would be a desert.*

This reply from an expert in the field encouraged me very much, and I was excited to think that I might have discovered something unique about the Canadian climate. I wrote to agricultural research stations in the NWT and the Yukon, and to the Central Experimental Farm in Ottawa, inquiring about crop production. I found that all the bulletins about crop production (gardens really) in the NWT mentioned the prevalence of drought. I read the results of soil surveys in the NWT.

While the pH of Ontario podsol soils range from extremely acid to moderately acid (pH 4.8-6.1), I found that the pH of Aklavik soils was 7.4-7.5, Fort Good Hope 7.5, and Norman Wells 6.8-8.0, indicating subhumid to semiarid climatic conditions. I agreed with Dr. Raup, that if it weren't for the permafrost, northwestern Canada would be a desert. I submitted my thesis on the limits of crop production in the Canadian Northwest to my advisors. The last hurdle to my Master's degree was the defense of the thesis which would take place in early June.

I also began to think about my future. What kind of job could I get? I enjoyed university life, and when Dr. Taylor wrote to me that the new Department of Geography at McMaster University in Hamilton was looking for a physical geographer, I was quick to apply. I was told that I had an interview at McMaster in May. I set out by train for Hamilton, but the train was delayed in Harrisburg, and I arrived hours late for my interview with the president. I don't remember much about the interview, except that I didn't get the job. Many years later, Lloyd Reeds, a friend of mine and a professor at McMaster, told me that the then-president George Gilmour told him that the reason I wasn't hired was because he thought a young female professor would be a distraction for the mostly male students at that conservative Baptist university!

In April, 1946, I received a letter from Bob telling me that he would return to Canada in May. I flew from Washington to Toronto to see him – my first airplane flight. Today it is hard to imagine that I was twenty-five years old and had never been in an airplane. We decided to be married in August. Bob applied to take dentistry at the University of Toronto, and we were very pleased that he was accepted as a second-year student (meaning a four year instead of a five year course). I was glad that I had not obtained the job at McMaster, since now I needed a job in Toronto.

I contacted Dr. Putnam who, like Dr. Taylor, always seemed willing to help his students. I knew that he was employed part-time at the Ontario Research Foundation working with Lyman Chapman on the physiography of southern Ontario. Dr. Putnam wrote to me some time later that he and Mr. Chapman had persuaded the director of the Foundation, Dr. Speakman, to hire me to work on the climatic requirements of pea production in Ontario. I knew absolutely nothing about pea production, and I don't think either Putnam or Chapman believed that my job would involve the climate of peas. I was told that my job would begin in September, 1946, at an annual salary of $2,000. I was thrilled with the thought that I would have a job doing research in climatology, and that I would be receiving such a large salary. Bob and I decided that, with my salary and his $80 per month as a veteran student, we could live quite well.

My thesis defense was scheduled for 7 p.m. one June evening. My committee members were Dr. Baker, Dr. Thornthwaite, Dr. van Royen, and a geology professor whose name I have forgotten. It was a most unusual experience. Shortly after the meeting began, the lights in the room went out, but Dr. Baker decided to continue in the dark. I have no doubt that the darkness shortened the questioning, and I was very relieved to be told that I had passed. I attended the convocation, and received my Master of Arts degree in Geography. I felt sad to leave College Park and the University of Maryland, but I looked forward to my career as a research scientist. Of course, it was also exciting to plan my wedding. I remember that before I left College Park, I went to New York to buy my wedding dress.

Although I had been a student at Maryland for only three semesters, it had been a most rewarding experience. I had gone to a foreign university, and had earned a Master's degree. I had met Dr. Thornthwaite and decided to be a climatologist, and bring his ideas of potential evapotranspiration and the water balance to Canada. I would be his disciple! He approved of my job at the Ontario Research Foundation and was my mentor and advisor for the four years I spent there. I didn't know until several years later, that he didn't approve of my marriage, thinking that it would interfere with my academic career. He gave me a reprint of his climate classification article with the inscription "To Marie, in the hope that it will inspire her to further service to science." I kept that reprint for many years. He was, without doubt, the most important person in my career, as these pages will show.

Bob and I were married in our family church in Chesley on August 3rd, 1946. The reception for about 30 guests was held on my parents' lawn. Bob and I went on a canoe trip in Algonquin Park for our honeymoon, and then spent the rest of the month at his family's cottage at Inverhuron on the shore of Lake Huron, near Kincardine. Bob's grandparents, who had lived in Pinkerton some 20 miles inland, had "discovered" Inverhuron in the early years of the century, and had built a cottage there. Their daughter, Bob's mother, owned this cottage in 1946 when I first visited. There was no electricity, so we used lamps, and no piped water, so we used the pump at the corner for drinking water, the lake for washing, and the privy at the back for the bathroom. The shoreline at the cottage was white limestone with a sandy beach nearby. The water was crystal clear. The cedar forest came almost to the water's edge, and the sunsets were fabulous. I think that I immediately loved Inverhuron, and it became my favourite place in the world.

CHAPTER 3
Research in Toronto and the Northwest Territories

Bob and I moved to Toronto in September, 1946; Bob to begin his dental studies at the University of Toronto and I to begin my job at the Ontario Research Foundation. We were very fortunate to have a place to live – an upper duplex apartment, fully furnished, on Palmerston Avenue, near Bloor Street. The house had belonged to my father's sister, who had recently died, and left it to my father. I think that we paid about $20 a month for this very nice accommodation. We knew we were extremely lucky, because rental apartments were very scarce in Toronto at the end of the war. There was street car service along Bloor Street, and the fare was about 8 cents. However, unless it was very cold, each morning we walked along Bloor; Bob to Spadina, then south to the Dental building on College, and I to University Avenue, then south to 79 Queens Park Crescent.

The Foundation occupied two houses on the east side of the Crescent, and I was given a desk in Lyman Chapman's office on the third floor of number 79. The mandate of the Foundation was to conduct scientific research for Ontario industries, and Mr. Chapman's group was the only one with an agricultural emphasis. Mr. Chapman and Dr. Putnam were then engaged in the mammoth task of writing *The Physiography of Southern Ontario* which would finally be published by the University of Toronto Press in 1951. The two men were old friends, having been classmates at the Ontario Agricultural College (now the University of Guelph). Since the 1930s they had been studying the landforms of southern Ontario, walking every road south of the shield, and unraveling the mysteries of the glacial deposits left by the last ice age. "Putty" was often in the office consulting with "Chappy" (as they called each other). Although they called me "Marie," I always addressed them as Dr. Putnam and Mr. Chapman.

Of course, Dr. Putnam's main job was at the Department of Geography, and I often walked over to Bloor Street to consult with him. Dr. Putnam continued to be the absent-minded professor. I recall that one day he took me by car to a meeting with the great Arctic explorer Steffanson. (He wanted me to ask the great man about the climate of Canada's Northwest Territories.) I don't remember much about the meeting, but I do remember returning to Dr. Putnam's car to find that his keys wouldn't open the door. A policeman helped him open the door somehow, but then, with a look of great surprise, Dr. Putnam said, "This isn't my car!" The Geography Department was expanding, as returning service men flocked to the university. I met some new members: Brian and Beryl Bird from Cambridge, Don Kerr from British Columbia and Jake Spelt from the Netherlands, all of whom had been hired by Taylor to help with the large numbers of geography students.

My life at the Ontario Research Foundation was very pleasant. All of the scientists wore white lab coats, so Mr. Chapman and I did also, although we didn't need them in our work. I enjoyed working with Mr. Chapman. He was a quiet, shy man who loved his work with Dr. Putnam. Both men were expert soil scientists, and realized the importance of climate in soil formation. They had written an article on the climate of southern Ontario in 1938, and were familiar with Dr. Thornthwaite's work. They suggested that my first research task should be to apply Thornthwaite's new classification of climate to the whole of Canada.

With Mr. Chapman's help, I found that the climate records (at that time climate data were the responsibility of the federal Department of Transport) were located in an old house on Admiral Road, north of Bloor Street, under the supervision of Morley Thomas. He was the only member of the climate section. Before the age of computers, of course, the temperature and precipitation records had to be copied manually. I found that there were 650 climate stations in Canada with temperature and precipitation data for at least 20 years, and these were the stations I used. The water-balance calculations also had to be done by hand, and I think each one required about 15 minutes of my time. But the results were very interesting. The stations in eastern Canada and the Pacific coast regions had no deficiency in an average year, while all the central Canadian stations had moisture deficits. The resulting map of moisture provinces showed humid climates in the east and west, subhumid in the Prairies and Northwest Territories (as my thesis had shown), and semiarid in southwestern Saskatchewan and southeastern Alberta, as Captain Palliser had rightly described the area in the 1800s.

I learned how to do the cartography for the climate of Canada research. There was a big drafting table in our office, and Mr. Chapman helped me with the design of the graphs and maps. It was a skill I made much use of in my career. He suggested that I send the manuscript to the journal *Scientific Agriculture* (now *Canadian Journal of Plant Science*) and they accepted it for publication in the September, 1948, issue with the title "The Climates of Canada according to the new Thornthwaite Classification." In the article I criticized the Köppen classification of climate: "Scientific geographers for years have sought a rational delineation of climatic regions since on it is based the explanation of vegetation and soil zones. Köppen's classification cannot explain the distribution of these phenomena because it is derived from them. The Thornthwaite method of using climatic statistics to arrive at a knowledge of the important factors in climate; water need, water surplus and water deficiency, although not perfect, represents an invaluable addition to Canadian climate research." (In 1986, I was asked to revise the maps, using metric units, for publication in *The Canadian Encyclopedia*.)

While I was doing the research for the climates of Canada article, I was also revising and shortening my thesis, since Dr. Thornthwaite had suggested sending it to the New York-based *Geographical Review* for possible publication. I sent the shortened version to Gladys Wrigley, the editor, in 1947, and it was accepted and published in 1948 with the title "Drought in the Canadian Northwest." I was thrilled to have a publication in this prestigious journal.

Dr. Thornthwaite visited the Ontario Research Foundation in 1947. He informed us that he had left the world of government science to become a consulting climatologist with Seabrook Farms, a very large vegetable-growing firm in southern New Jersey. As perhaps the first consulting climatologist in the United States, Dr. Thornthwaite successfully advised Seabrook Farms on their planting and irrigation scheduling, and the disposal of wastewater. He had also established a "Laboratory of Climatology" in nearby Centerton for research in climatology, and for the design and production of meteorological instruments. He discussed with Mr. Chapman and me the possibility of actually measuring potential evapotranspiration in the Toronto area. He had earlier worked with Contreras Arias in Mexico in designing equipment, called an evapotranspirometer, to actually measure this important climatic parameter, and had tested this equipment at his new Laboratory of Climatology. Mr. Chapman and I were excited about this new project, and with Dr. Thornthwaite's help we designed equipment that would be easy for me to maintain. The problem in an urban area like Toronto was to find a large open location close to the Foundation where the evapotranspirometers could be installed. Mr. Chapman was (amazingly) successful in obtaining permission to install the equipment in an undeveloped area of Mount Pleasant Cemetery! The principle of the evapotranspirometer was simple: to keep a grass-covered area supplied with water by sub-irrigation, and to measure the daily water use. It was assumed that the plants would use all the water they required and that the water used (PE) would depend solely on atmospheric conditions. Thornthwaite's definition of PE was "the amount of water that potentially would evaporate and transpire from a vegetated surface if an optimum amount of water was continually supplied."

(I found out years later that "potential evapotranspiration" was also being researched in the 1940s by two other well-known scientists: Howard Penman in England and Mikhail Budyko in the Soviet Union. The three did not know of each other's research, because the war prevented the exchange of scientific information. It seems amazing that the three scientists, in three different countries, were independently exploring the concept of PE at the same time.)

The equipment for the Mount Pleasant research consisted of four large tanks (five ft. square and three ft. deep) sunken in the soil, with a layer of gravel below a sandy loam soil. Two of the tanks were planted with drought-resistant crested wheatgrass, and two were planted with timothy, a grass believed to have a high moisture requirement. Above ground was a water-supply mechanism, which allowed water to flow to the tanks as it was used by the vegetation. There was an overflow mechanism that measured excess rainwater. The area around the tanks was planted with grass to avoid any oasis effect. The installation was completed in May, 1947, and I began to take daily readings in June, causing considerable interest among the gravediggers. More than once, they asked me what I was doing, and I think were mystified when I said I was measuring potential evapotranspiration!

When readings were discontinued because of snow in mid-November, the total PE for the timothy tanks averaged 394 mm, and 392 mm for the crested wheatgrass, while computed PE was 450 mm. Of course, we informed Dr. Thornthwaite of the results, and he and Mr. Chapman encouraged me to submit my results to the *Canadian Journal of Research* (published by the National Research Council). My paper was accepted and published in August, 1948 with the title "An Experiment to Measure Potential Evapotranspiration," my third published paper that year. In the abstract, I stated, "A method of obtaining daily values of the potential evaporating power of the atmosphere was used for the first time in Canada in 1947. The results verify Thornthwaite's formula for computing PE in Southern Ontario." Even the director of the Foundation, Dr. Speakman, admitted surprise that the two very different grasses used similar amounts of water, and he became very supportive of my research. I continued the experiment for another two years with continued good agreement between measured and computed PE. The final report was submitted to the *Canadian Journal of Research* and published in October, 1950 as "Three Years of Evapotranspiration at Toronto."

In 1948, Mr. Chapman and I discussed with Dr. Thornthwaite the possibility of taking the experiment to an Arctic location. Dr. Thornthwaite was very keen to obtain PE data for a high-latitude station, and I was very excited about the possibility of visiting Arctic Canada, after my research on drought in the Canadian Northwest. There were two major problems. The first was that my employer, the Ontario Research Foundation, was not interested in funding research in Canada's north, and the second was the problem of who would take the readings after installation of the evapotranspirometers. We discussed a possible location for the experiment. Dr. Putnam suggested that we ask for advice from Tuzo Wilson, a professor of Geophysics at UofT, and a member of a team who had walked across the NWT from Hudson Bay to the Mackenzie River the year before. Tuzo Wilson, whose name later became very well-known for his continental drift theory, gave us very helpful advice. He suggested Norman Wells on the Mackenzie River, just below the Arctic Circle, as the best location, since it had an airport where planes large enough to carry our equipment could land. He also informed us that Norman Wells was an Imperial Oil Limited (IOL) company town, and suggested that we should contact them.

We first needed a grant to buy the equipment, and to pay for its transport to Norman Wells. I had heard of the Arctic Institute of North America, with offices in New York and Montreal, and in the fall of 1948 I applied to them for a "Grant in Aid of Research." Mr. Chapman and I were pleased when I received a letter from Pat Baird, director of the Montreal office, stating that I had been granted $1200 to "measure potential evapotranspiration in Norman Wells, Northwest Territories." One of the conditions was that I should obtain the co-operation of the Department of Transport, whose Meteorological Branch operated Canada's climate stations. Of course, Mr. Chapman and I had already realized that, and had gone to see the director of the Met. Branch, Andrew Thomson, in his office on Bloor Street. Mr. Thomson said that he thought the project very important, and would give us all possible co-operation. He agreed that the equipment could be installed at the Norman Wells airport, and that the Met. Observer, Alan Shaw, would take the readings after I left. He wrote a long letter (a copy of which I still have) to the District Controller in Edmonton detailing the help to be given to me. One paragraph stated:

Mrs. Sanderson will require some assistance in installing the equipment, taking the readings, and for transportation back and forth to the airport. In view of the importance of the work, the understanding of the water balance at high latitudes, I feel we should do our utmost to ensure its success.

Our next task was to approach Imperial Oil Limited, and we were very pleased with the results. IOL offered to fly me to Calgary and then to Norman Wells on a company plane, and to let me live in the company residence and eat in the company dining room while I was installing the equipment – all for no charge.

By May, 1949, the plans were finalized, and the equipment sent by commercial aircraft to Norman Wells. I was very excited at the prospect of seeing the Northwest Territories, the area that I had written about in my MA thesis. On June 11th, Alan Shaw sent a message that the equipment had arrived safely, and on June 14th I was on the Imperial Oil Lockheed Lodestar aircraft en route to Calgary. The Lodestar was a twin-prop aircraft that was used by IOL for both passengers and freight. I was airsick since the flight took most of the day, and I had never been on such a long flight before. But for a geographer it was a fabulous experience to see Canada from the air for the first time. Nothing had prepared me for the sight of the Rocky Mountains as we approached Calgary. I actually cried at their beauty. The next day we flew on to Edmonton where I had a meeting with the Department of Transport officer in charge of the Norman Wells airport.

Finally we took off for the long flight to Norman Wells at latitude 65° N. I was the only passenger on the flight, and the pilots, Gordie Latham and Jim Keir, let me sit in the cockpit for a while. It was a clear day, and the view was fantastic, as we left the world of farms and roads behind, and saw the northern landscape of lakes and trees. We landed to refuel at Hay River on Great Slave Lake, and soon saw the majestic Mackenzie River. At 4,240 km, the Mackenzie is Canada's longest river, and has the tenth largest river basin in the world. It is navigable from Great Slave Lake to the Arctic Ocean. It was a long flight, as we followed the Mackenzie River northward, until we finally saw the town of Norman Wells on the east bank of the mile-wide river, and landed on the gravel strip of the Norman Wells airport. The small settlement owed its existence to the discovery of oil in the area in the 1920s, and a refinery had been established. During the Second World War, the Canol pipeline and accompanying road had been built by the Americans to take oil from the Norman Wells refinery to Alaska.

"The Wells" was a company town, and seemed strange to my eyes. There was one (unpaved) road to the airport, wooden sidewalks, no schools, stores or churches, and I think, only two private houses. Mr. Mackenzie, the IOL manager, and his wife lived in one of the houses, overlooking the river, with quite a large garden. I met Mrs. Mackenzie, and we became good friends. She was interested in my research, and eventually became a volunteer observer for the Thornthwaite Lab, growing peas and measuring and reporting their growth.

I was given a room in a building with other IOL employees, and ate my meals in the communal dining hall. I found that there was no problem hitching a ride from the town to the airport where the meteorological office was located. I met Alan Shaw, who was to take responsibility for the experiment when I left. He was a very nice person, although I very much doubt that he was excited about measuring potential evapotranspiration. My first job was to install the large tanks which we had decided to place at the edge of the runway to avoid the permafrost. No-one was interested in digging holes, but I finally persuaded the Radio Range staff to excavate the holes with a bulldozer. The tanks were planted with Kentucky bluegrass, recommended by the Department of Agriculture because of its resistance to winter-kill. With warm temperatures in June, the grass in the tanks grew quickly and daily readings began on July 2nd. The equipment functioned very well.

I found the Norman Wells environment fascinating. The landscape was so different from anything I had seen, so immense and so unpopulated. The midnight sun took some getting used to, but that was part of the area's mystique. The temperatures were quite mild, as I had expected from my earlier work with the climate data. Daytime highs occasionally reached the low 80s, but warm temperatures brought out the mosquitoes. I had been warned about the mosquitoes, but they were much worse than I had imagined. One had to cover every inch of exposed flesh with repellant when outdoors.

One weekend, a group of us hiked along the abandoned Canol highway, a very interesting experience, since the bridges had been washed out, and we had to ford the very swift and cold mountain streams while roped together. We also hiked in the Franklin Mountains, east of Norman Wells. One evening, at 10 p.m., the IOL pilots flew a group of us to Kittygazuit for a baseball game! This settlement in the delta of the Mackenzie River at 69° N had an RCAF Loran (long range aid to navigation) station which had been established in 1947. I remember that there was only one female in the settlement and she was so pleased to see another woman, that she wanted me to stay for a few days. This was also my first view of the Arctic tundra. There are no trees beyond this settlement, just tundra as far as the Arctic Ocean at Tuktoyaktuk. On another occasion, we flew north to Fort Norman, one of the oldest settlements along the Mackenzie, where we visited the Hudson's Bay store and the Anglican Church.

An Imperial Oil photographer took my picture at the research site in Norman Wells in July 1949. It was published in The Imperial Oil Review. (Photo with permission from the Imperial Oil fonds, Glenbow Archives, Calgary, Alberta)

The Mackenzie River at "The Wells" was always a scene of busy activity, with the Northern Transportation Company Limited (NTCL) tugs pushing their long lines of barges up or down river. NTCL was then a crown corporation (it is now Inuit owned), that provided transportation for freight to the settlements on the river and along the Arctic coast. At that time (1949) there was little activity in oil and gas exploration north of Norman Wells, and the new settlement of Inuvik, in the Mackenzie Delta, had not yet been built.

On July 25th, with the equipment working well, I felt that I should return to Toronto. I felt sad to leave the Northwest Territories, but very happy with the success of the evapotranspiration experiment. I kept in touch with Alan Shaw, who continued the readings until September 2nd, when a storm flooded the equipment and disconnected the pipes. For the 62 days of record, the measured amounts of potential evapotranspiration for the two tanks were 234 and 232 mm, and the computed amount was 230 mm – very good agreement. Of course, Mr. Chapman and Dr. Thornthwaite were pleased with the results. I submitted my report to the Arctic Institute, and also wrote an article, which I sent to the *Geographical Review*. It was accepted, and published in the October, 1950, issue, with the title "Measuring Potential Evapotranspiration in Norman Wells, 1949." My conclusion was that the poleward extrapolation of the Thornthwaite formula for computing the potential loss of water from a vegetated surface to the atmosphere, gives results of the right order of magnitude. Many years later, in *A Bibliography of Canadian Climate 1763-1957*, author Morley Thomas stated that my PE experiment at Norman Wells was the first climate experiment conducted in Canada's Arctic.

Topics other than evapotranspiration occupied me in1950, my last year at the Foundation. Putnam and Chapman had written an account of the climate of southern Ontario in1938, and they suggested that I update the article, and add the element of variability to the usual discussion of climate normals (30 year averages). I used data from 83 stations in southern Ontario, the area south of North Bay, and prepared maps of the usual parameters of seasonal temperature and precipitation. In addition, I showed the variability of these parameters over a period of 26 years, for four representative stations: Harrow, Guelph, Ottawa and Walkerton. The resulting paper entitled "Moisture Relationships in Southern Ontario" was published in *Scientific Agriculture* in June, 1950.

For the four years that we spent in Toronto, Bob, of course, was busy with his dental studies. He had been out of school for three years, and found it very hard to become a student after his experiences in World War II. We looked forward to the summers, when we could spend weekends at Inverhuron. I remember that during Bob's final year, when he was allowed to do dental work on real people, I took advantage of the free clinic, and had my wisdom teeth extracted.

Bob graduated from the Faculty of Dentistry in June, 1950, and we had to decide where he would set up his dental practice. I very much wanted to live in a university city, so the only choices in Ontario in 1950 were Toronto, Kingston (Queens), London (Western) and Windsor (Assumption College, run by the Basilian fathers and affiliated with Western). I was inclined to choose London, but my husband's uncle, Hardie Campbell, a medical doctor in Windsor, persuaded us to come to that city. Bob was excited at the prospect of actually practicing dentistry, but I felt sad to leave my exciting job at the Ontario Research Foundation. In those days there was no question of the priority of my husband's career. Also, I was approaching 30 years of age, and we had to consider starting a family. So in June, 1950, we left Toronto for a new life in Windsor. I think that I always knew that some time in the future I would return to my geographic career, but it would have to wait a while.

CHAPTER 4
A Stay-at-Home Mom, and a Student Again

In July, 1950, we moved to Windsor, and Bob set up his dental practice on Ouellette Avenue. He told me that it was a great feeling, at age 29, to be finally earning a living. I felt strange not going to work every day, but realized that my personal life now had to take precedence over my life as a research climatologist. We wanted a family, and were delighted when our daughter Susan was born in April, 1951. We bought a house in the suburbs on Randolph Street, and I adjusted to being a stay-at-home mom. Son Hardie was born in 1953, and James in 1955. I was certainly busy as a mother and housewife, but could not entirely forget my climatic research. I kept in touch with Dr. Thornthwaite, and he suggested that I become an associate researcher with his Lab. A technician from Centerton came to Windsor, and installed two evapotranspirometer tanks in our backyard. I requested a Stevenson screen and rain gauge from the Meteorological Branch, and became an official Canadian weather observer. For the five years we lived on

Randolph Street, I sent my weather observations to the Met. Branch, and my evapotranspiration data to the Thornthwaite Lab.

Dr. Thornthwaite had been successful in convincing the Seabrook Company to use his climatological expertise in the planting and harvesting of their vegetable crops. It was perhaps the first successful application of applied climatology in the world. I was invited to the Laboratory of Climatology in Centerton several times during the 1950s. I was excited to see the interesting climate research being done, and thrilled to meet the famous climatologists invited to the Lab by Dr. Thornthwaite. One such eminent scientist was Rudolph Geiger, the associate of the famous climatologist Köppen. Many years later, on a trip to Germany, I visited Dr. Geiger at his home in Munich, and he told me that Thornthwaite had literally saved his life. After World War II, food was very scarce in Germany, and Dr. Thornthwaite had sent food parcels which kept the Geiger family alive. I also met Russ Mather, a research scientist at the Lab, who had been a PhD student of Dr. Thornthwaite's. Russ and I formed an immediate friendship, since we both felt that we were Thornthwaite's disciples. Russ, and his wife Amy, became lifelong friends, and I often stayed at their home on my trips to the Lab during the 1950s and 1960s.

I also kept in touch with the geographers at UofT. I heard that Griffith Taylor would retire in 1951 to return to Australia. I was invited to his retirement party, but had to decline because of the birth of my daughter, Susan. I was also invited to the inaugural meeting of the Canadian Association of Geographers at McGill University in 1951, when Griffith Taylor was named Honorary President, and Dr. Putnam was elected the first President.

Bob and I enjoyed living in Windsor. Although it was a small city, it had all the advantages of the huge metropolitan area of Detroit with its three million people, just minutes away by tunnel or bridge. We shopped at Hudson's, a fabulous store then located in downtown Detroit, and, like most Windsorites, smuggled our purchases back to Windsor. We took the children to the excellent Detroit Zoo, the Detroit Institute of Arts and the many museums, including the Ford Museum in Greenfield Village. We often drove to Detroit to take the boat trip to Canadian Bob-Lo Island with its fabulous amusement park. There was excellent theatre in Detroit, and the Metropolitan Opera came to the Masonic Temple for a week each spring.

In 1956, we were shocked to hear that my husband's brother had died in an automobile accident. Since his wife had died previously, Bob and I decided to adopt his two daughters Sharon and Joan. Our house in suburban Windsor was not large enough for our expanded family, and we moved to a lovely spacious house on Willistead Crescent in old Walkerville. It was located across from Willistead Park and Willistead Manor, the stately mansion built by Hiram Walker of the whiskey-making firm in the early 1900s. It had become a library and art gallery in the 1950s. I loved our house on Willistead, which I would call home for the next 27 years. I found that looking after five children and a big house left me little time for any intellectual endeavours, yet I yearned to continue my education.

In 1959, I persuaded Bob that I should take an evening course, entitled "The Geography of Oceania" given by the Department of Geography of the University of Michigan at the Detroit Institute of Arts in downtown Detroit. The lecturer was Peter Gosling, who knew the area intimately, as he had been there during the war. I enjoyed the lectures about an area I knew absolutely nothing about, and I enjoyed being back in a university atmosphere. The next year I discussed with my husband the possibility of enrolling in the doctoral geography program at Michigan. He said that I had "put him through dental school," and that he had promised to return the favour some day. This involved paying my tuition at Michigan, and hiring a housekeeper for the days I would spend in Ann Arbor. Bob was years ahead of his time in agreeing that his wife should continue her education. I was very happy to give up my housekeeping chores, and our housekeeper, Barbara, became an important member of our family for 24 years.

I had an interview with Dr. Davis, the chair of the Department of Geography at the University of Michigan. Charles (Bud) Davis had a long association with the university. His undergraduate and graduate degrees in geography were from Michigan, and he was an instructor, professor, and then head of the department until 1966. He helped bring the department into the space age through the development of computer mapping and the use of remote sensing. He was a friendly and likeable person. He said he would be honest with me, that they had accepted women PhD candidates before, but none had finished the program. I replied, in no uncertain terms, that I intended to finish, and he believed me. I am sure that the letter to Dr. Davis from Dr. Thornthwaite (excerpts below) helped:

> *During the last five years, Marie has been busy with her children, but she has not lost touch with the intellectual life. You will probably have other sources of information on her publications. She had ten papers that I know of between 1948 and 1950 and these papers have had an enormous influence in Canadian agricultural climatology and continue to be quoted.*
>
> *I hope that you will accept her as a graduate student. I have no doubt that she will be able to resume just where she left off five years ago. She may wish to work on a climatic problem. If you should want assistance from me or a member of the Laboratory staff, we will do what we can.*

The Geography Department of the University of Michigan accepted me as a graduate student, and kindly made my timetable convenient, requiring my presence on campus only three days a week. Luckily for me, the interstate highway system in Michigan made my trip from Windsor to Ann Arbor only one hour long. Bob bought me a Mini Morris, a little station wagon that took me to Ann Arbor for the five years of my doctoral work with no problems.

During the years 1960-1963 I took eight courses. I was the only female in all my classes. I especially remember two of the courses. Professor John Nystuen lectured on "Quantitative Methods," a new field of geography in the 1960s, and a new topic for me. My favourite course was George Kish's "History of Cartography." Kish was an inspiring lecturer and imparted to his students his love of old maps. Of course we were fortunate to have on campus the Clements Library, the repository of one of the best map collections in the United States. We often had classes in the Clements and were allowed to see and even touch (with gloves on) 16th- and 17th-century maps by such famous cartographers as Ortelius and Blaeu; even a letter from Columbus to Queen Isabella.

In 1963, I was informed by Dr. Davis that three preliminary examinations were required to be accepted as a candidate for the PhD degree. The first was entitled "Regional and Topical Geography." The purpose of this oral examination was to evaluate the student's general geographic knowledge. I will never forget that day in November, 1963. The more advanced students had told us what to expect. In addition to the general questions from the panel of four professors, there was an unusual twist. The student was asked to throw a dart at a wall map, and discuss the physical and human geography of the region so identified. There were three students (two men and I) taking the exam that day. The first very nervous student was ushered into the examination room, only to reappear a few moments later – he had fainted! I was the next person called and, not surprisingly, found that I couldn't even remember my name. The committee members were sympathetic, and gave me a few moments to collect my thoughts. Since they knew that my field of geography was climatology, many of the questions concerned Thornthwaite's climate classification and water-balance studies. These I had little trouble with. My problems came when I threw the dart at the map. It landed on the Kamchatka Peninsula in Siberia, an area that I knew nothing about. I desperately tried to think of a homoclime (a place with a similar climate). I must have made some sense, since I was informed that I had passed the exam.

The second part of the comprehensive exam was challenging, and very unusual. I was given a topic, in the form of a question, on a Thursday afternoon, and had to hand in a written report on the following Monday. My question was, "Is Windsor a suburb of Detroit?" I rushed to the library to find definitions of the word "suburb" and found that they included, for example: "the number of people living in the suburb who worked in the central city" and "the amount of automobile traffic between the suburb and the central city." I had Friday and Saturday to do the research, and Sunday to write the report. I rushed around to the various agencies in Windsor and Detroit to collect the necessary data. I applied the appropriate criteria. My husband kindly looked after the children while I typed my report. I concluded that Windsor qualified as a suburb of Detroit in all the criteria, except for the problem of the international boundary. My professors liked my report and I received an A grade.

The University of Michigan also required PhD candidates to have a reading knowledge of two foreign languages; to translate a certain number of pages in a certain amount of time. Dictionaries were permitted, and we were allowed to choose the books. For my German exam I chose Rudolph Geiger's *Das Klima der Bodennahen Luftschicht* (The Climate of the Layer of Air Near the Ground) – a monumental work. I thought that since the book was about climate, it would be easy to translate. I was wrong! I found out how complex scientific German could be. I failed in my first attempt, but managed to pass the second time. I'm afraid that I never used my knowledge of German in my scientific career. Luckily, because of my high school French, I had no problem with the French exam. The university notified me in December 1963 that I was accepted as a PhD candidate in Geography.

While a student at Michigan, I kept in touch with Dr. Thornthwaite. In 1961, as President of the Association of American Geographers, he was asked to give the presidential address at Michigan State University in East Lansing, and invited me to attend. It was my first AAG meeting. Dr. Thornthwaite's talk was entitled "The Task Ahead," a plea for geographers and especially climatologists to be more quantitative and more scientific. Sadly, it was the last time that I saw my friend and mentor. He contracted bone cancer the next year and died on June11, 1963. He was only 63 years old.

In November 1963, as the world remembers, President Kennedy was assassinated. The Department in Ann Arbor was devastated and I also felt a personal sense of loss. I sent flowers to the Department and received a very kind letter from Dr. Davis:

> *The flowers you sent were lovely and much appreciated. Even more appreciated was the spirit that moved you to do it. As a pro-American you are our favorite Canadian, and we send our affectionate thanks for your thoughtfulness.*

During my years as a student, I was busy with my family and my courses, but I also love to travel. Fortunately Bob shared this interest, and with his dental practice flourishing, we now had the funds to indulge our passion for seeing the world. We tried a cruise in 1960, leaving New York on the German ship "Bremen" for two weeks in the Caribbean. I found that, like my maternal grandmother, I was not a good sailor, and was almost immediately seasick. I spent most of the time at sea on deck staring at the horizon! But the places we visited were fascinating: Charlotte Amalie in the Virgin Islands, Jamaica, Martinique, Curacao,

Venezuela, and the Panama Canal. It was the first and last cruise I have taken. Thank heaven for aircraft.

In 1962, Bob and I had a five-week tour of Europe. In those days, a tour of Europe was considered a once-in-a-lifetime experience, and our opportunity came with a tour organized by the Ontario Dental Association. Living in Windsor, we always used the Detroit Airport, only 30 minutes from our house. I remember that we flew to New York to board the TWA (Trans- World Airlines) flight to Prestwick in Scotland. It was my first trip abroad, and I was very excited to visit the countries of Europe that I had studied in my geography courses. When we landed in Prestwick, Bob and I left the tour for a day to visit a cousin of his who lived in a suburb of Glasgow called Bearsden. We found a taxi and gave the driver the address, only to have him reply – with an accent we had trouble understanding – that he had never heard of the place. After many attempts to communicate, we finally wrote "Bearsden" on a piece of paper. Evidently we weren't pronouncing it correctly. An interesting welcome to Scotland!

We went by bus through England, stopping at York to see the cathedral, and Cambridge to tour the colleges. In Cambridge, a highlight for me was a visit to the Scott Polar Research Institute, where we saw artifacts from Scott's famous 1910-1911 Antarctic Expedition. We saw the list of the scientists who accompanied Scott, with the name Griffith Taylor, of course, among them. His salary was listed as £250.

We spent a few hectic days in London, staying at the Regent Palace Hotel – with the bathroom down the hall. We were taken to most of the historic sites: the Tower of London, Westminster Abbey, Buckingham Palace and the changing of the Guard, St. Paul's Cathedral and the British Museum. We flew to Cologne in Germany, where Bob attended an international dental convention. We had a cruise on the Rhine. Then it was on to Switzerland and the Alps. We enjoyed the trip to the top of the Jungfrau, being inside a glacier, and even a ride with a dog team. We went by bus through the Brenner Pass to Italy where we were entranced by the splendours of Florence, Venice and Rome. In Rome, I shall never forget the thrill of seeing the opera "Aida" at the Baths of Caracalla, and exploring the Forum and St. Peter's Basilica. We took an overnight train to Paris, where we visited the Louvre, the Opera and Versailles, and saw the Folies Bergère. The final stop was

Copenhagen in Denmark. It was an exhausting trip, and we looked forward to a relaxing flight back to New York. Unfortunately, this was not to be. Just two hours after take-off, while we were being served dinner, the plane suddenly dropped a few thousand feet, sending food and trays flying. Some people screamed. I was sure that we were going to crash into the ocean, but after what seemed a long time (probably only seconds), the plane resumed its forward motion. Evidently it was "clear air turbulence" which I had never heard of, and luckily, never again experienced. As a result of this long trip, Bob and I developed a love of travel in Europe. In 1964, we visited France, Holland and Belgium. Bob very much wanted to see the actual location where he had been captured during the war, and we explored the area in eastern Holland without success. He concluded "They've paved the roads, the hedges have grown, and my memory has faded."

Back in Windsor, the next problem in my pursuit of a PhD was the dissertation topic, and I decided to investigate a hydrological problem of personal interest to me. Since my marriage, I had spent my holidays at Inverhuron on Lake Huron, and like all Great Lakes shoreline residents, was fascinated by the changing lake levels. Every spring, the first question everyone asked was, "Is the lake higher or lower than last year?" My various uncles and aunts informed me that there was a seven-year cycle in lake levels – up for seven years, then down for seven years. As a geographer I had trouble accepting this, and as the 1960s was a period of falling lake levels, I decided that finding out what caused these changes would be an interesting topic for a dissertation. Since Lake Erie was closer to Windsor (and Ann Arbor) than Lake Huron, I decided to focus on the changing levels of Lake Erie. But who would be my advisor? There were no professors of climatology or hydrology in the department. Finally, John Nystuen kindly agreed to supervise my research. Other members of my committee were Mel Marcus (a glaciologist, recently appointed to the Geography Department), Donald Portman (a professor of meteorology at Michigan, and Dieter Brunnschweiler (a climatology professor at Michigan State University). It was a very prestigious committee.

My timing was most fortunate. Lake Erie, like Lake Huron, had rapidly declining levels in the early 1960s, and there was much interest in the causes of this decline. The media often blamed the seven-year cycle, or the diversion out of Lake Michigan at Chicago. My first task, of course, was to find out about the hydrology of the Great Lakes, and the history of lake levels. Luckily for me, the U.S. Corps of Engineers, responsible for monitoring lake levels and river flows in the United States, had an office in Detroit, and they were most helpful. They gave me graphs of Lake Erie levels (from 1918) which showed that during the period of record, the difference between the extreme high and low levels was five feet, a very large amount. The lowest recorded level had been in 1936.

Keith Rodgers of the Great Lakes Institute at the University of Toronto also provided me with much information, as did Morley Thomas, Jim Bruce and Lloyd Richards of the Meteorological Branch, Department of Transport. I found out that the Great Lakes are indeed a unique feature; the only system of such tremendous size in the whole world, owing its existence to the melting glaciers of the last ice age. Since the levels of the lakes are so important for navigation and hydro-power development, gauging stations had been established at many locations on the shores of the lakes, as well as in the connecting rivers, in both Canada and the United States.

I read everything I could find on the causes of the changing levels. From my research, I discovered that the level of Lake Erie, as with the other lakes, varied in response to mostly climatic factors: the precipitation on the surface of the lake, evaporation from the lake surface, the runoff from the drainage area, and the difference between the inflow from the upper lake and the outflow to the lower lake. For Lake Erie, this can be represented by the equation

$$S = I - O + P + R - E$$

where S is change in storage (change in level), I is the inflow from the Detroit River, O is the outflow through the Niagara River, P is the precipitation on the lake, R is the runoff from both the Canadian and U.S. portions of the basin, and E is the evaporation from the surface of the lake. I decided to express all the variables in terms of months and in inches of depth on the surface of the lake. Imperial units were used, since the data in both Canada and United States were in the Imperial system. I decided that my observation period would be 1959 - 1964.

The S, I and O data were relatively easy to obtain from U.S. Corps of Engineers, and the Canadian Hydrographic Service (the Canadian agency which operates the gauges around the perimeter of the lake, and in the Detroit and Niagara Rivers). Runoff from the drainage area was more difficult to determine since, in the 1960s, only about 70% of the drainage area had measured stream flow data. For the ungauged areas, I used the Thornthwaite water-balance method to compute monthly runoff for the 60 months of my observation period, using temperature and precipitation data for the 133 climatic stations in the basin. There were no computers then, so all the computations had to be done manually. Monthly runoff into Lake Erie from the land areas of the basin was found to vary a great deal, from 0.1 inches on the surface of the lake in October, 1962 to 8.8 inches in April, 1959.

Quantifying over-lake precipitation was also a problem. Researchers had attempted to estimate the ratio of over-water to over-land precipitation, but in the literature there was little agreement on the ratios. I decided to use a geographic method to solve the problem. I plotted monthly precipitation amounts for the 60 months of my study period for the 133 stations, and drew isopleths across the lake. I then could determine the monthly volumes of water, and consequently the depth of precipitation on the surface of the lake. This was time-consuming, of course, since I had to repeat the process for each month of my study period. Next was the problem of determining monthly evaporation from the surface of the lake. The literature contained various formulae for estimating evaporation using meteorological data from shore stations. However, humidity values were needed, and these were not available for my Lake Erie basin stations. I decided that the only thing to do was to solve for E as the remainder in the water-balance equation, quoted above. (The monthly change in level was the result of the inflow minus the outflow plus over-lake precipitation plus land runoff minus lake evaporation.) Thus, transposing the equation:

$$E = I - O + P + R - S$$

All the parameters were expressed in inches over the surface of the lake so it was easy to solve for monthly E. I found that annual evaporation values varied greatly, from 22.0 inches in 1959-60 to 39.6 inches in 1961-62.

The resulting "net basin supply," the amount of water contributed to the Great Lakes system by the Lake Erie basin, varied from 32.0 inches (on the lake surface) in the first year of the study, to 1.5 inches in the last year, a very large difference. This concept of net basin supply was new to me, and made me realize how important it is to consider each lake basin separately. Each of the four basins (Superior, Michigan-Huron, Erie and Ontario) is unique, with vastly different climatic and land-use characteristics. The Lake Erie basin is the most southerly and warmest, with the least precipitation and the most agriculture of the basins. Lake Erie basin's declining net basin supply in the early 1960s explained the rapid lowering of Lake Erie. Lake Erie's record low level in 1964 has not been surpassed as I write in 2009.

I decided to write a letter to the editor of the *Windsor Star* to enlighten readers about the true causes of the low levels. They printed my letter, but in an editorial it was stated that "the science is interesting, but Great Lakes residents KNOW that there is a seven-year cycle in the Lakes." I was also eager to talk about my findings with my relatives at Inverhuron; that the declining levels were the result of the weather, little precipitation and runoff and increased evaporation. I'm afraid that I never convinced them that there was no seven-year cycle.

I finished writing my dissertation in early 1965 and submitted it to my committee. They recommended a few changes, and the defense was scheduled for May, 1965. Of course I was very nervous as I drove to Ann Arbor for the meeting, but the defense went well. Each member of the committee asked me questions, which I found easy to answer. Dr. Portman's first question was, "When will you be ready to go on a lecture tour?" They all congratulated me at the end and wished me well.

The date of my convocation was December 18, 1965. Bob agreed that a celebration was called for, and we sent invitations to my professors for a dinner at our house in Windsor. However, this did not occur, since the week before convocation, Bob was taken to hospital with a heart attack. (Luckily he was able to be home for Christmas.) He insisted that the children and I go to Ann Arbor for the occasion. It was a memorable day. I drove with four children, ages 10-14, to a friend's house in Ann Arbor for lunch before the ceremony – hot dogs and champagne (for me). I found that my rented gown was too long, and had to spend some time shortening it. We finally drove to the parking garage for the convocation ceremony, where I promptly drove into the side of the building. Too much champagne! We were so late that the children had to sit in the second balcony, where they could hardly see the graduates far below. The BA and MA candidates only stood when their names were called, while the PhD candidates did go to the platform to receive their degrees. It was a very beautiful ceremony with music and flowers – my third convocation. It was quite a wonderful feeling that I was now Dr. Marie Sanderson. I had certainly enjoyed my years at Michigan, but I looked forward to having another career – that of a university professor. Luckily for me, there was a university in Windsor, where I was to spend the next 23 years of my life.

CHAPTER 5
A Professor of Geography

The University of Windsor received its charter as an Ontario university in 1963 during the period of expansion of the Ontario university system. Already in existence on the site was Assumption College, formerly affiliated with the University of Western Ontario. Assumption, a teaching college of the Catholic Order of Basilian fathers, remained a part of the new University of Windsor. Francis Leddy was appointed the first president and I had attended his installation ceremony in 1963. I met Paul Vandall, then the only professor teaching geography. He advised me that the new university would be expanding quickly and would need geography professors. I also met Tony Blackbourn, a University of Toronto graduate, appointed in 1964. Both urged me to apply for a position in the fall of 1964, although I had not yet received my degree. I wrote to Dr. Leddy and to the Dean of Arts and Science, Father N.J. Ruth, enquiring about a teaching position. I also had the foresight to write to geography professor Ken Hare, whom I had met while at the Ontario Research Foundation, and who was then teaching at King's College, London, asking for a letter of reference. Ken replied that he would write to Dr. Leddy whom he knew.

Things moved very quickly, and on November 30 I received a letter from Dr. Leddy asking me to come for an interview. I vividly remember that interview. I was very nervous, since I had never had any teaching experience. I mentally rehearsed what I would say about geography and my special interest, climatology. I needn't have worried. The interview lasted perhaps five minutes. One question Dr. Leddy asked "Do you plan to have any more children?" When I replied in the negative, he told me that I was hired. I received a letter in December, 1964, informing me that I was to join the "Section of Geography" as an assistant professor in September, 1965, at an annual salary of $8,000. This seemed an incredible amount in my eyes.

The University of Windsor is situated in the western part of the city, south of the Detroit River, and almost beneath the Ambassador Bridge to Detroit. In 1965, it had about 5,000 students. My office was in the basement of the Social Sciences building, and the geography lecture rooms were in the same building. That first year I was asked to teach a climatology course, a geomorphology course, and a Geography of Canada course. I was happy to teach the climatology course, but it had been a long time since I had read any geomorphology. I felt that I knew the geography of Canada fairly well – but how to teach it was a different matter. That summer I spent a lot of time in the library. I remember very well my first lecture. I had prepared my notes, and practiced reading them. Lectures were to be 50 minutes long, and I thought that I had enough material. Of course, I was very nervous, and probably spoke much too fast. When I reached the end of my material, and looked at my watch, I was horrified to note that only 35 minutes had passed. I'm sure the students were pleased, however.

Naturally, my favourite course was the second-year climatology course, because I considered myself primarily a climatologist, and I like dealing with numbers. That first year there were about 30 students in the climatology class, and only five were female. This ratio of female/male students never seemed to change during my teaching career. For some reason, females didn't seem to like climatology. I decided not to recommend a text, since I could not find one that agreed with my concepts of climatology, but I gave my students lots of references and also provided them with photocopied handouts. I think that my syllabus was a good one. I always began by explaining the difference between weather and climate. I defined weather as "the current state of the atmosphere," while I said that climate, usually defined as "average weather" should really be described as "the study of the exchanges of heat and moisture at the surface of the earth." This was the definition that Dr. Thornthwaite had taught.

My lectures focused on the three important balances controlling the climate at the earth's surface: the radiation balance, the energy balance and the water balance. I spoke first about the sun, the source of all the earth's energy. I explained how the short wave radiation from the sun was affected by the earth's atmosphere, some reflected back into space by clouds, some absorbed by clouds and particles, with only about 50% reaching the earth's surface. I spoke of the importance of the reflectivity (albedo) of the surface, with snow reflecting about 90% of the short wave radiation back to space, and water reflecting only about 5%. Because the earth has a much cooler temperature than the sun, the radiation leaving the surface is in the form of long wave radiation. Some of the long wave radiation is absorbed by clouds and water vapour and gases such as carbon dioxide, and re-radiated back to the earth. (Water vapour is the most important greenhouse gas, while carbon dioxide is a very minor greenhouse gas.) This process is called the "greenhouse effect," since it keeps the earth warmer than it otherwise would be. The result of all these radiation exchanges at the surface of the earth is called the net radiation.

The second great balance is the energy (ability to do work) balance. Net radiation may heat the surface, heat the air and evaporate water. For example, in a desert, with no water available, the net radiation heats the surface and the air above the surface. If water is available, as in a humid climate, much of the net radiation is used to evaporate water. The third great balance is the water balance. Much of the earth's surface is covered with water, and the earth cannot gain or lose water. It is continually being recycled in a process called the "hydrological cycle"; evaporation from water (and land) into the atmosphere, condensation in the atmosphere to form clouds, precipitation from the atmosphere onto the earth's surface, and runoff from the surface back to the oceans.

In my lectures, of course, I also told my students of my own climate research, especially the evapotranspiration experiments in Mount Pleasant Cemetery and in Norman Wells. They certainly became familiar with the name Thornthwaite and his water balance model. I spoke about the climate classifications of Köppen and Thornthwaite. I described my research on Lake Erie levels. Since the university was located on the Detroit River, which my students saw every day, I spent some time on the hydrology of these unique Great Lakes.

I don't think that I was a very good lecturer. I was always nervous before my classes, and I know that I spoke too quickly. I varied the curriculum by inviting visiting speakers, and taking the students on field trips. That first year I invited my former doctoral committee member, Mel Marcus from the University of Michigan, to speak to my class on his work in the Icefield Ranges Project in the Yukon. What a fabulous lecturer! One of my students that year was John England, who later became one of Canada's outstanding glaciologists. I arranged a field trip for the students in my "Geography of Canada" class to the Clements Library in Ann Arbor, where they were shown the earliest maps of North America. I took my climatology class to the federal Agricultural Research Station at Harrow, near Windsor, where researcher Jim Fulton showed them his lysimeters (which measured actual evapotranspiration), research of great interest to me. We also visited the meteorological office at the Windsor Airport, so the students could see how weather data were obtained and transmitted. I persuaded the Meteorological Branch of the Department of Transport to establish an official Canadian weather station at the university. This they did at a vacant lot on campus, and I required my climatology students to take the daily readings. This was not a popular activity in winter. Many years later I found out that some students, especially those from warmer climates, would acquire the necessary data by phoning the airport weather office. I suppose I should have expected this.

My job also required that I do research, and this aspect of my work I liked very much. One of my projects at the Ontario Research Foundation had been a study of the climates of Canada, including drawing a map of water surplus (surface runoff) of Canada for which I had used the Thornthwaite water-balance technique. This topic still interested me, especially after reading in newspaper articles in 1965, that Canada had one-third of the world's fresh water resources. I wondered how this figure had been obtained, and wrote to the federal Department of Northern Affairs and Natural Resources for clarification. The reply I received was that the estimate was based on Canada's share of the volume of the Great Lakes, plus the volume of all other lakes. This seemed to me to be a very inaccurate estimate of water resources, since the vast amount of water in the Great Lakes is not a renewable resource, but a gift of the last ice age. In my mind, Canada's water resources should be the annual surface water runoff.

I asked the Meteorological Branch for funds to derive estimates of this runoff by using data from all the river gauging stations in Canada, supplemented by estimates for the ungauged areas using the Thornthwaite water-balance technique. I was awarded $2,600 for this research, and I was thrilled to be again involved in a research project. The money was used to hire a cartographer, and a student to do the actual water-balance computations. The student I hired to do this was my best student that year, David Phillips, who was to become Canada's best-known climatologist. The research was published by the Meteorology Branch in 1967 as "Annual Average Water Surplus in Canada." The publication showed annual average surplus by province and for the whole country. We found that the total for Canada was 2.8 million cubic feet per second (cfs), omitting the Arctic islands where no data were available. The estimate for the world's water resources at that time was 40 million cfs, making Canada's share of the world's water resources about 7%. I think that our article was the first to suggest this figure which is often quoted in scientific publications today – 40 years later.

Scientific publications were important to advance my career, so I was very pleased to have my dissertation on Lake Erie water levels published by the Thornthwaite Laboratory's "Publications in Climatology" in 1966. My friend, Russ Mather, had taken over the directorship of the Lab after Dr. Thornthwaite's death in 1963. A summary of the dissertation was also published by the "International Association of Great Lakes Research" in its "Proceedings of the Ninth Conference on

Great Lakes Research" which was held at the University of Michigan in 1966. Since my doctoral thesis had been on a Great Lakes topic, I had joined this interesting organization in 1965.

In my second year at the University of Windsor, I felt a little more comfortable with my lecturing, and I continued to ask my geography friends as guest lecturers. Peter Gosling from the University of Michigan, and Dieter Brunnschweiler from Michigan State University were kind enough to come that year. I also took my climatology students to the Detroit offices of the U.S. Corps of Engineers to see how the lake level data were obtained.

When my classes ended in May, Bob and I felt that we deserved a holiday. That year there was a dental convention in Beirut in Lebanon, and we decided to see that part of the world, visiting England before, and Greece and Italy after the conference. England was special for me on that trip because we went to Greenwich to see the Prime Meridian and the Harrison chronometers. (These instruments were the actual ones, designed by Harrison, to solve the problem of determining longitude.) We flew to Beirut where we stayed at the beautiful St. George Hotel right on the shore of the Mediterranean. We enjoyed the conference at the American University, and the visit to the Beirut Casino, one of the most beautiful in the world. We visited the ancient cities of Byblos and Baalbeck. I was thrilled with the visit to Greece – to actually see the Acropolis and the Agora, and the National Museum where we purchased a replica of the head of the "Boy from Marathon." We rented a little red convertible and drove to Delphi, that most sacred place in Greek mythology, and all around the Peloponnesus, to Naphlion and Mycenae and the great theatre at Epidaurus, where Maria Callas was to perform later that month.

In May 1968, we visited Portugal and Spain; our first trip to that area. We drove from Lisbon to the Algarve in the south, and as far west as one can go in Europe, to Cape St. Vincent, where Prince Henry the Navigator had his school in the 15th century. In Spain, we visited Madrid and the famous Prado museum, Toledo and the Costa del Sol. Our favourite place was Granada and the fabulous Alhambra, that beautiful Moorish castle which was returned to Spain by Ferdinand and Isabella in 1492. We saw the statue of Columbus showing Queen Isabella his map of the new world.

Back at the university, I continued to apply for research funding, and in 1968 I received $3,000 from the Meteorological Branch of the Department of Transport for a study of the variability of annual runoff in the Lake Ontario basin, as part of an international research effort entitled "International Field Year in Lake Ontario." The field year on Lake Ontario in 1972 was part of the International Hydrological Decade, and my study was to provide background information on runoff. Since the gauged data were sparse, I used the Thornthwaite water-balance technique and the climate data for 81 stations in and near the basin (with unbroken records of at least 30 years), to estimate the historical runoff. I found that annual runoff was normally distributed, and I drew maps of the variability of this important parameter for the Lake Ontario basin. Of the three factors in the lake's net basin supply; precipitation, evaporation and runoff, runoff was the largest factor, contributing 47-58 inches to the surface of the lake annually. My paper was published in *Water Resources Research*, a publication of the American Geophysical Union, in June 1971 with the title "Variability of Annual Runoff in the Lake Ontario Basin."

As a member of the Canadian Association of Geographers, I found out that the International Geographical Union (IGU) was to meet in New Delhi in India in December 1968. I applied to the National Research Council for travel funds to attend the conference to present a paper, and was pleased to receive a grant of $1,470. It was my first long trip alone. I remember that I wore a hat and white gloves. (In 1968 that was appropriate apparel for a woman traveller.) I can still recall that first smell of India (cow dung, curry, human perspiration) when arriving in early morning in New Delhi. I stayed at the beautiful Ashoka Hotel. There were 1,800 delegates at the conference, and the impressive opening address was given by Indian President Indira Gandhi. Most of the attendees were men, with the exception of the Soviet delegation which had several women delegates. I met Maria Gavrilova, a climatologist from Yakutsk in Siberia who spoke English very well, and who became a good friend. The Canadian delegates were entertained at the beautiful Canadian Embassy, and were taken for dinner by UofT professor Ali Tayyeb. A highlight for me was a trip to the Taj Mahal with fellow Canadians, Tony Blackbourn and Gordon Merrill. We stayed in Agra long enough to see the Taj Mahal by moonlight, an unforgettable sight! The IGU meetings left something to be desired in the way of organization, but for me, it was a chance to meet geographers, and especially climatologists, from around the world. I met Dr. Davitaya, a climatologist from the Soviet Republic of Georgia, (a tall elegant man who chaired one of the climatology sessions), Dr. Sekiguti from Japan, and I renewed acquaintance with Dr. Subramanian (Sube), an Indian climatologist whom I had previously met at the Thornthwaite Lab.

I had signed up for a post-conference field trip to south India. The ten-day trip started in New Delhi and ended in Madras, with at least a day each in Bangalore, Mysore, Cochin, Trivandrum, Madurai, Trichinopoli and Madras. We travelled some 2,000 miles for a total cost of $180, an incredible bargain! We were met at each city by local geographers, who were wonderful guides, but I think I saw enough Hindu temples to last me a lifetime. We stayed at interesting guest houses. I remember one particular occasion when our Indian hosts asked if anyone played tennis. Four of our group replied in the affirmative, and a match was arranged for 8:00 a.m. the next morning. We had three assistants, an umpire who called out the score after each play, and two ball-boys. Since all four of us were quite mediocre players, it was a hilarious game. However, after four weeks of travel in India, I found the poverty in the country most depressing, especially the children who followed us, pulling at our clothes and asking for money or food. I have never returned to India.

On my return trip to Canada, I stopped for a few days at Tehran in Iran. It was in the days of the Shah, and tourists were still welcome. I stayed in the beautiful Hilton Hotel, where there were Christmas trees and children singing Christmas carols. The tours of the palace and the crown jewels were unforgettable. I especially remember a large sphere depicting the world, completely covered with jewels: diamonds for the equator and the tropics, sapphires for the oceans, and rubies for the continents. I wonder what has happened to these priceless treasures. I also stopped in Rome for a few days. I again visited St. Peter's to look at the Pieta, and also managed to attend an opera. I was pleased to find, after this long trip, that I was quite capable of traveling alone.

In the late1960s, the University of Windsor grew rapidly, and geography was granted the status of a department in 1966. Jack

Ransome was hired as chair of geography, and in 1967, Amrit Lall and Gustavo Antonini were new appointees. Jack was an American urban geographer with a degree from Harvard, who remained at Windsor until his retirement. Amrit was an Indian geographer, who taught cultural geography, and whose relatives I visited in India. Gustavo remained at Windsor only a year before taking a position at the University of Puerto Rico. There were now six members of the department, and we got on very well together. We began to have parties on special occasions with our geography major students. I recall the Christmas party in 1968, when the students roasted the professors. David Phillips roasted me with a skit he entitled "High Heels in the Tundra" since I always wore high heels in class, and everyone knew of my love of the North.

In 1968, Ihor Stebelsky, a Toronto graduate, joined the department, and remained until retirement. The year 1969 saw the largest expansion, when five new people were hired: Alan Trenhaile, Placido LaValle, Vern Smith, Ron Seale and Tony Brazel. Smith and Seale remained for only a few years; LaValle stayed until retirement; and Trenhaile also stayed, later becoming head of the department. Tony Brazel was a climatologist, a student of Mel Marcus at Michigan, but he didn't remain at Windsor long, following Mel to Arizona State. In 1970, two more professors were added: Stewart Raby, who stayed only a few years, and Gerald Romsa, who stayed until his retirement. My courses also changed as time went on, although I taught the second year climatology course until I retired. I no longer taught Geomorphology or the Geography of Canada, but added a course on the History of Geographical Thought, a topic I had been interested in since taking a course on the subject from George Tatham. I taught that course until I retired. I was also given the responsibility of the fourth-year seminar course. The department required fourth year students to do theses involving original research, and I enjoyed guiding them through this final requirement for the BA degree in Geography.

In June 1969, and again in 1970, my friend Russ Mather, then Chair of Geography at the University of Delaware, organized a summer course in climatology, sponsored by the U.S. National Science Foundation. Russ asked me to be one of the instructors, to give lectures on my research in Windsor. Ken Hare (then at Toronto), and Bob Muller of

Louisiana State were also visiting professors. It was a great experience for me to have graduate students from all over the States, who were very interested in climatology. Russ' department at Delaware flourished and inaugurated a PhD program in climatology in the 1970s.

In May 1970, Bob and I were traveling again – this time to Germany. I took the opportunity to visit Rudolph Geiger at his home near Munich. Geiger was then a frail old man, but his English was still very good, and he told me that he was "still working on his beloved climatology." He spoke of his association with the great Vladimir Köppen. He told me of his special regard for Thornthwaite, and his trips to the Laboratory of Climatology. I told him that I had used his book, *Das Klima der bodennahen Luftschicht* for the foreign language requirement for my degree at Michigan. I didn't tell him that I had to try the exam twice! It was a very emotional visit with this dedicated scientist.

Also in 1970, I began exploring the idea of a research field other than water, and thought of actually measuring radiation, using the radiation equipment we had purchased to obtain real data, something I had not done since my evapotranspiration experiments. I submitted a proposal to the National Advisory Committee on Geographical Research to "Measure rural and urban net radiation in Windsor," and it was accepted. My radiation results were published in the McGill University *Climatological Bulletin* in 1974 as "A Preliminary Radiation Climatology of Windsor, Ontario."

During the early 1970s, I was also engaged in a research effort measuring precipitation in Windsor and the surrounding Essex County, to determine the effect of a large metropolitan city (Detroit) on precipitation in the downwind area. I obtained funding from the Meteorological Branch for a three-year study. Precipitation, both rain and snow, was collected in Belfort-type precipitation gauges, which measured precipitation by weighing it, and recording the amount on a chart. We enlisted the help of farmers in the county, and they (or more often their wives) were very good observers. I remember that personnel at the world headquarters of Hiram Walker, situated on the banks of the Detroit River, also took readings for us. We found that precipitation did indeed increase downwind from a large city, and our results were published in the *Journal of Applied Meteorology* in 1978 with the title "The Effect of Metropolitan Detroit-Windsor on Precipitation."

In 1970, I also began work on a very interesting assignment. Brian Bird at McGill had been asked to be the General Chairman of the next IGU to be held in August 1972 in Montreal, and he asked me to organize the sessions on climatology and hydrology. I began to plan a very extensive program, hopefully improving on the sessions that I had attended in New Delhi. I wrote to climatologists I knew in Canada and internationally, inviting them to be session chairmen for the conference in Montreal. It was an impressive list, a "Who's Who" in climatology and hydrology at the time: Helmut Landsburg from the University of Maryland, Ken King of Guelph, Ken Hare of Toronto, Peter Adams of Trent, Morley Thomas of Environment Canada, T. Sekiguti of Tokyo, F. F. Davitaya of the USSR, Heinz Lettau of Wisconsin, Arleigh Laycock of Alberta, and, of course, Russ Mather of Delaware. The above scientists (all men of course) acted as chairs for the 12 sessions and assisted me in inviting good speakers. It was a very successful IGU, with some 1,000 attendees, and I think the sessions in climatology were very good. The closing session in honour of Dr. Thornthwaite was very moving for all who had known him. The week-long conference was certainly a highlight of the year for me.

Since I had been appointed as a professor at Windsor in 1965, I was due for a sabbatical leave in 1972. With my job at the IGU finished, I was free to plan my sabbatical. I had always dreamed of studying at Oxford or Cambridge universities in England, and I wrote to Jean Gottman, the Head of the School of Geography at Oxford, to inquire if I could spend some time as a visiting scholar at that university. He agreed, suggesting Halifax House, a graduate residence, as a place to stay. I also applied for a grant from the British Council, under the Commonwealth University Exchange Program. This was a very smart move, since it entitled me to visit several British universities while I was in England during the fall of 1972.

My proposed research for my study leave was to work on a biography of Mary Somerville, the first female geographer in England (probably in the English-speaking world), who lived from 1780 to 1872. I had heard about her in the course on historical geography given by George Tatham at the UofT, and her life interested me. Biography has always been my favourite reading and this would be my first attempt at writing a biography. Unfortunately, when I contacted the Bodleian Library, where the Somerville papers were stored, I was told that another researcher had been given permission to use the papers, and I was not allowed to see them. I had to be content to view only her published work.

I had an interesting time in Oxford. I explored the colleges and museums, and was given a library card for the Bodleian Library – quite an honour. The geographers at the School of Geography were very nice to me. Margery Sweeting arranged for me to be a fellow at St. Hugh's College, at that time still an all-female college. I was invited to Somerville College (named for Mary Somerville) for dinner one night, and was amazed to find that the students, at least the ones I met, didn't know who Mary Somerville was.

Since the train trip from Oxford to London was only an hour long, I often went into the city to explore the sights or go to a show. I particularly remember one occasion at the Oxford station. I was walking on the station platform, waiting for the train, when I saw another walker, whom I thought I recognized as a geographer. When he came near me, I said "I think I recognize you. Are you not a geographer?" He answered "No, I am a Canadian." This rather puzzled me, so I replied "I am a Canadian also, and I think I met you at a geography conference." To this, he stated "No, I am the Prime Minister of Québec." (He was Robert Bourassa, then the Premier of Québec.) He didn't appear to be very friendly, but his companion, who turned out to be his bodyguard, did speak to me, telling me that Mr. Bourassa had been visiting Keble College in Oxford, where he had been a graduate student. I certainly felt embarrassed, but then realized that it was quite a humorous incident.

I spent a lot of time in the Bodleian Library. I read Somerville's books: *On the Connexion of the Physical Sciences* published in 1834, which she dedicated to Queen Victoria, and her most famous book *Physical Geography* published in 1848, which had seven editions. She was an amazing woman, entirely self-taught, since in those days women were not allowed to attend university. Women's brains were not thought to understand science, and Mary's father discouraged her interest in science saying, "Remember Mary T. – she went quite mad studying latitude and longitude." However, Mary was encouraged by her husband, Dr. William Somerville, a member of the Royal Society, who introduced her to the famous scientists of the day: the Herschels, Roderick Murchison, Charles Lyell, Sir Francis Beaufort, as well as the explorers James Ross, William Parry and John Franklin. This was the period of great debate over the creation of the world, and Mary's candid support of Lyell's scientific views caused her to be publicly censured from the pulpit of York Cathedral. She corresponded with the famous German geographer, Alexander von Humboldt, and was very impressed with his great work *Cosmos*. She was awarded the Victoria Medal of the Royal Geographical Society in 1869. The Royal Society commissioned a bust of her to be placed in their Great Hall. It was (and still is, I imagine) on view at the Royal Society offices in London, even though she was never invited, because she was a woman, to become a member of that illustrious society.

Since I didn't have enough material to write a book about this interesting woman, I decided to do an article, which I submitted to the *Geographical Review* in New York after I returned to Canada. It was published in July 1974, with the title "Mary Somerville; her work in physical geography." I wrote in the introduction that Mary Somerville has been called "the first woman scientist in English history." She wrote the first textbook on physical geography in the English language. Her *Physical Geography* was published in 1848, three years after Alexander von Humboldt's famous *Cosmos* appeared, and before geography was recognized as a university discipline in England. Her remarkable life spanned almost a century, from 1780 to 1872. It was an exciting century for science, with great strides made in astronomy, geology, meteorology and geography, and Mary Somerville understood and commented on all the great discoveries. However, it is interesting that she believed, like most of her generation, that women's brains were not suited for the physical sciences. I have often wondered what she would think of the women scientists of today.

My time in Oxford came to a very pleasant ending in mid-December 1972. My husband, with daughter Susan and son Jimmy flew to London, and we travelled to Filzmoos near Salzburg in Austria for a skiing vacation. We were not an accomplished family in this sport, but we had skied in central Michigan. It was our first ski trip to Europe, and we found that the Alps were certainly more exciting than the hills in Michigan. We enrolled in classes at the local ski hill, where we had to contend with rope tows and t-bars. Of course, we had trouble understanding the instructions in German (to Susan "Follow your Bruder"), but we loved the scenery and the local customs. The food was fabulous at our hotel. Christmas Day in Filzmoos was exciting, with real candles on the Christmas trees. When our holiday ended, we received medals for passing our ski tests.

In the early 1970s, Bob and I found that Mexico was a nice place for winter holidays. At first, we flew to Mexico City and drove to Acapulco, since at that time there were no direct flights from Detroit to the Pacific coast of Mexico. We stopped one time in Taxco, a lovely city noted for its silver mines. Another time, it was Patzcuaro, where we there was a fabulous local market. At that time, Acapulco was the only resort on Mexico's Pacific coast, but in a few years, other holiday destinations were developed, and we holidayed in Puerto Vallarta and Ixtapa. We also explored more of Europe. At the end of one school term in May, we visited the island of Majorca in the Mediterranean, and the island of Ibiza the following year. In 1973, we explored the beautiful city of Dubrovnik and the Adriatic coast of (then) Yugoslavia.

The summer of 1973, at the end of my sabbatical year, was special. I had a trip to the Northwest Territories, my first since my Norman Wells days. Our daughter Susan had graduated from the University of Western Ontario in June with a degree in geography, and with four friends (three females and one male) planned to canoe the length of the Mackenzie River from Hay River to Tuktoyaktuk, some 1,200 miles. They agreed that I could join them in Inuvik and canoe with them for the last leg of their trip. Susan and her friends drove to Hay River with a canoe and kayak in July, and had a wonderful and accident-free trip down the Mackenzie River to Inuvik. I flew there in August to join them. We departed for "Tuk" under clear skies with warm weather, and almost 24-hour daylight. It was quite nostalgic for me to see the mighty Mackenzie River again. In Inuvik, the river enters the delta with many distributaries flowing north to the Arctic Ocean. It was easy paddling. We had an amazing encounter the second day out. We saw a tent and people, the only other campers we saw on the trip, and when we paddled over, I saw that they were people I knew – Brian and Beryl Bird from McGill.

Our first campsite on the shores of the Mackenzie
River near Inuvik, August, 1973

The delta of the mighty Mackenzie where it empties into the Arctic Ocean

On the third day, the weather changed and became quite cold and
windy. The river is wide and soon built up sizeable waves, forcing us to
make camp and wait for better weather. After two days of inactivity, we

decided to continue our trip, although the waves were so large that my stern paddler said "Mrs. Mackenzie (as they called me), stop paddling and start baling." Even so, we were shipping water, and decided to make for shore to assess the situation. Our map showed that we were near the Imperial Oil camp called "Bar C." We managed to reach this outpost of civilization, and my daughter went into the camp, and evidently asked if her mother and her friends could spend the night. Such unbelievable hospitality we received! We were cold and wet, and were given hot meals and warm beds. In the morning, with the wind still blowing, the manager suggested that we be flown to Tuk on the company helicopter. Of course we accepted, and arrived in Tuk in style, with the canoe and kayak also on board the helicopter.

Tuktoyaktuk is an interesting settlement of several hundred Inuit on the shore of the Beaufort Sea. It is in real tundra country, since there were no trees after Bar C. We were taken on a tour of the Distant Early Warning (DEW) Line station just outside the town. There were at least 80 of these stations along the 70th parallel in Canada and Alaska, built by the United States military during the 1950s at the height of the cold war. Tuk also boasted a very busy Northern Transportation Company Limited (NCTL) terminal. We stayed at the only "tourist" hotel, a small house owned by Dr. Swartz of Montreal. We made our own meals. We visited the famous pingo (an ice-cored hill that forms in permanently frozen ground), and were shown how the local residents used it as a refrigerator. When it was time for us to leave, the kind people at NTCL arranged for us to be flown to Edmonton on the company plane – at no cost.

During the mid-1970s I continued my interest in the Great Lakes, and attended the annual International Association for Great Lakes Research (IAGLR) meetings. I was pleased to hear that my friend Jim Bruce had been instrumental in persuading the federal government to build a centre for lake research in Burlington, Ontario, called the Canada Centre for Inland Waters. He was its first director. In 1974, I took my climatology class to visit this unique institution. When Tony Brazel left the University of Windsor to go to Arizona State University he was replaced by John Jacobs, a climatologist from the Institute of Arctic and Alpine Research in Boulder, Colorado. I found that John and I shared similar interests, not only in climatology but also in the Arctic.

An interesting initiative in climatology occurred in the 1970s, due largely to Ken Hare at Toronto. It was called "Friends of Climatology"; climatologists from Ontario and Quebec, who met once a year to discuss current research and who nominated a climatologist each year to be an "orbiting climatologist." I was invited to be the "orbiter" for 1974-75. I travelled to 14 campuses and spoke to students in geography, biology, environmental science, microclimatology and physics, about the research we were doing in urban climate at Windsor. I began with the Atmospheric Environment Service in Downsview and my friend Morley Thomas; then to the University of Waterloo and Jim Gardner; to Montreal where I visited Concordia and Don Fraser, then McGill and Ben Garnier, Rick Wilson and John Lewis. After Christmas, it was the University of Guelph with Ken King and Terry Gillespie of Land Resource Science; then McMaster with Wayne Rouse, John Davies and Hank Hannell. I spent three days in Toronto where I visited the campuses at Scarborough and Erindale (now Mississauga) for the first time, and my old *alma mater*, the main campus at UofT with host Ken Hare. Later it was back to Waterloo and Wilfrid Laurier University with Gerry Hall; then to Queen's with Harry McCaughey, and to Carleton with Mike Smith. My last stop was Brock in St. Catharines with Tommy Thompson. (Readers will note that not one of the climatologists I visited was female. I have often wondered why climatology does not appeal to women.) In recalling that experience, I realize that the "Friends of Climatology" was quite a unique idea, bringing together climatologists from many disciplines to discuss common problems. It was an idea ahead of its time. What an influence it could have had in these days of concern about global warming.

Since the IGU meetings in Montreal in 1972, I had kept in touch with several Soviet climatologists, in particular F.F. Davitaya in Tblisi. In 1974, he wrote to me suggesting that I apply for funding to visit climate researchers in the Soviet Union. I applied for an NSERC (Natural Sciences and Engineering Research Council) grant, co-sponsored by the Soviet Academy of Science, to visit three Soviet climatologists: F.F. Davitaya in Tblisi, Georgia; Maria Gavrilova in Yakutsk, Siberia; and M.I. Budyko in Leningrad (now St. Petersburg). My application was accepted, and I left Canada in October 1975 for three weeks in the USSR.

My flight was from Detroit to Moscow, where I was met by an Intourist guide and taken to the Academy of Sciences hotel. (Throughout my entire trip I had Intourist guides, usually very attractive young women, who were also my interpreters.) My guide helped me to register at the hotel, and left, telling me she would see me in the morning. However, I was not ready to go to bed, and was eager to see something of Moscow, so I decided to take a bus to Red Square and see the sights. After walking around impressive Red Square, I went for dinner at a near-by hotel. It was dark when I finished dinner, and I realized that I didn't know how to return to my hotel by bus, so I decided to take a taxi. This turned out to be a problem; there were lots of cabs going by empty, but none would stop for me. I began to be worried, until a young man approached me and said in very good English, "May I call a cab for you?" I thanked him, and then realized that he was quite inebriated, as he walked unsteadily into the busy traffic, waving his arms at oncoming taxis. One did stop (or would have run him down), and with a deep bow to me, he said, "I want you to think well of the Russian young people." Another interesting observation on the Soviet system occurred the next morning at breakfast, when my guide said to me, "Did you enjoy Red Square?"

My few days in Moscow were full of activities; seeing the Kremlin, and many museums and palaces. I enquired about my meeting with Dr. Budyko, but this never happened. An unforgettable event was a night at the opera to see Giselle. The opera was superb, but more interesting was the intermission. I saw a beautiful room, tables with cakes and bottles of champagne, and people eating and drinking, but no sign of any waiters. I found someone who spoke English, and asked him how one got served? His reply was, "Just help yourself, and when you leave, tell the cashier what you had." I couldn't believe it. I doubt that the practice continues today.

Then it was time for me to leave on the long Aeroflot flight to Yakutsk in Siberia. After many hours of flying (and no food on the flight), the plane landed at Irkutsk on Lake Baikal, six time zones from Moscow, where I was to change planes for the flight north. I realized what a huge country the Soviet Union was, since it occupies twelve time zones, and Irkutsk was only half-way. One unusual aspect of air travel in the Soviet Union was that all flights operated on Moscow time. It was surprising to learn that my flight north was to leave at 4:00 a.m. local time, when I thought it would be a civilized 10:00 a.m. departure. I had a 22 hour wait in Irkutsk! I was very eager to visit Siberia, to see differences and similarities between the Canadian and the Soviet north. I was also looking forward to seeing Maria Gavrilova and the Permafrost Institute. The flight north stopped at quite a few places, and I was worried that I wouldn't know when we reached Yakutsk, since all the announcements were in Russian, of course, and I couldn't read the Russian signs at the airports. I needn't have worried. When it seemed that we must be near the North Pole when we landed yet again, I saw outside my window, on the tarmac, Maria with several others, with huge bouquets of flowers, waving up at me. It was an indication of the wonderful hospitality that I was to receive in Siberia.

Yakutsk at 62° N is similar climatically to Yellowknife, NWT, but while Yellowknife then had fewer than 10,000 people, Yakutsk had 160,000. It is an old settlement, founded in the early 17th century by Russian explorers in their search for a route to the Pacific Ocean. There were some lovely old wooden houses, but also many large ugly Russian-style apartment buildings, built on piles sunken into the permafrost, as in Canada's north. Yakutsk borders the Lena River, which is very similar to our Mackenzie River. It is surrounded by the hemlock and birch forest, the taiga, so beloved by the Siberian people. I stayed at the Lena Hotel, a very comfortable hotel, with triple doors and windows to protect against the Arctic climate.

As in Moscow, I had an interpreter who went everywhere with me, starting with breakfast each morning in a private dining room at the hotel. My days were extremely busy. There were visits to the Permafrost Institute, the many branches of the Siberian Division of the USSR Academy of Sciences, the Geological Museum, the Biological Institute, and the botanical gardens, where I was proudly given a locally-grown apple. I was driven out of the city to see pingos and thermokarst lakes, similar to those I had seen in Canada. I remember with pleasure a luncheon in my honour at Dr. Gavrilova's summer house outside the city. The house, although not the land, was owned by the Gavrilovas, and the excellent lunch was made by Maria's husband. At the lunch, as I found everywhere in the USSR, there were copious amounts of vodka and Soviet champagne. After lunch, we danced on the wide verandah of the "dachau."

We visited the University of Yakutsk and the Geographical Society of Yakutia, but I did not meet any students. I was told that they were helping the local farmers with the potato harvest. One day the Institute arranged a field trip for me and my interpreter, to the Ordzhonikidsevskiy region, south of Yakutsk, to the small village of Povrovsk. It was a 100 km trip over very bad roads, but it turned out to be a most interesting day, a step back in time. The houses were of brown wood, and the streets unpaved. I was told that I was the first Western woman to visit the village, and I noticed that little children hid behind their mothers when they saw me. I was taken to see an agro-meteorological station and the botanical gardens. I was surprised to see that most of the town officials and the scientists were women. There was a luncheon in my honour, with more than 100 guests, and toasts to Canada which we drank in large wooden goblets filled with kumiss, fermented mare's milk. I still have the goblet that was given to me that day.

The director of the Permafrost Institute had sent their research ship to Povrovsk to take our party back to Yakutsk, and I really enjoyed the trip on the Lena River. There seemed to be much more traffic on the Lena than on the Mackenzie, with not only tugs pushing long lines of barges loaded with lumber, oil drums and machinery, but also a good number of pleasure craft. My guide told me that she and her husband had canoed 1,200 miles down-river to the Arctic coast, and was pleased to hear that my daughter had done a similar trip on the Mackenzie. On my last night in Yakutsk, the director had a farewell dinner for me in his apartment, and everyone escorted me to the airport afterwards – at 4:00 a.m. The return trip to Moscow took 21 hours and was exhausting. I found that the poorly pressurized aircraft caused my ears to hurt and left me deaf for several days, but everywhere I was impressed with the consideration of my fellow travellers. I was always escorted to the front of the line.

From Moscow I travelled 1,400 miles southeast to Tbilisi in the Republic of Georgia, to visit F.F. Davitaya and the Institute of Geography. Again, I was made aware of the huge size of the Soviet Union and its many climates, as we left cold Moscow and arrived at the beautiful city of Tbilisi with its Mediterranean climate and palm trees. The Georgians often refer to their republic as "Trans-Caucasia" situated as it is on the Koura River between two ranges of the Caucasus Mountains. The city had more than one-million inhabitants and a proud history of more than 2,000 years.

I was in Tbilisi for eight days, and each day was crammed with activity. I was usually picked up each morning by Dr. Davitaya with an Institute car and driver. (I found that in the Soviet Union it was very rare for private citizens to own cars.) I spent one day at the Institute of Geography, of which Dr. Davitaya was the director. The high status of geography was obvious; the Institute had some 300 employees and 60 research scientists with a stress on applied research. Another day I visited the university and the Geography Department, and was told that there were 400 students majoring in geography. I was taken to the Hydrometeorological Institute where Dr. Davitaya had worked as a weather observer, as had another well-known Georgian, Joseph Stalin.

One of the most interesting days was spent visiting Kaheti province and a hail-suppression station, 200 km east of Tblisi in a wine-producing area. Wine is widely grown in Georgia, and evidently there is much damage to the vineyards from hailstorms. The hail-suppression program in Georgia was a large enterprise and very impressive. The station we visited employed 500 people in a very military-like setting. The chief method of hail suppression was the shooting of rockets containing chemicals into the storm clouds to change the hail into rain. The scientists I met were convinced of the efficiency of the program, but I'm afraid there was little proof that this was so. The cost to the state must have been enormous, but wine is a very important commodity to Georgians. At every meal I was urged to try the local wines or champagnes.

I had a most unusual experience on my last Sunday in Tbilisi. A young colleague of Dr. Davitaya took me on a tour of the city, and asked me if there was anything special I would like to see. I knew that the communist government had closed most of the churches in the USSR, so I asked my guide if any church in Tbilisi was open. He took me to a beautiful Russian Orthodox cathedral, where we joined a few elderly female worshippers, and listened to lovely Gregorian chants. It was quite a moving experience, and when we were outside he said to me, "Thank you for allowing me to see something in my country that I have never seen." Obviously, for the sake of his career, he would never have gone into the church alone. Another comment that I remember hearing from several Georgians was "Our country has always been overrun by others. Right now it is the Russians – but that will change." In 1975, I had no idea how correct that statement was to be.

My three-week trip to the Soviet Union was a fascinating experience. I was very impressed with the people I met in Yakutia and Georgia, and the fact that they were so enthusiastic about their work. Many of the scientists were women, which was very different than the situation in Canada. I learned a little about the communist system and how the people dealt with it. Many scientists resented the fact that they could not travel outside their country, and some of the women mentioned the fact that they couldn't buy nice clothes. Actually, all the clothes, for both men and women, seemed to be of very poor quality. I never did find out why the visit to Dr. Budyko was cancelled, and I never met that distinguished scientist who resembled Dr. Thornthwaite in many ways.

I enjoyed my academic travel, but I also liked travelling with my husband for pleasure. One of our friends recommended Colombia in South America as an interesting place to visit, and in 1974, we had a pleasant holiday in the capital city of Bogota, and Cartagena on the Caribbean coast. We had been warned to watch out for thieves in Bogota, but we had no problem. Cartegena was a beautiful city, and I recall our visit to the historic old fort. We visited Colombia again the next year, to stay at Santa Marta on the Caribbean. We had a most unpleasant experience during the taxi ride from Cartagena to Santa Marta. A little convertible car was approaching us when it suddenly went off the road, crashed into a hill, turned over, and the driver flew out of the car, and actually bounced on the road in front of us. Our driver stopped (we thought to help), but instead he robbed the man lying on the road, and then put him in our taxi. We decided it would not be wise to be in a car with a dead man, especially when we could not speak Spanish, so we got out of the taxi. This all happened very quickly, and as we stood on the side of the road, we realized that the taxi had driven off with our luggage in the trunk. A kind Colombian motorist gave us a lift, perhaps because he thought we were related to the dead man. We tried to tell him to follow the taxi, but neither Bob nor I knew the Spanish words. Bob finally tried the word "morgue."

Our Good Samaritan seemed to understand that word, and kindly took us to the Santa Marta morgue, where luckily we found the taxi with our luggage.

After that rather unpleasant holiday, it was good to be back at my job at the university. It seemed that there was always something to look forward to. This time it came in a letter from Dr. Davitaya in Tblisi, inviting me to chair a climatology session at the up-coming IGU conference in Moscow in August 1976. I hadn't thought of visiting the Soviet Union so soon after 1975, but part of the conference was to be a pre- conference Symposium on Polar Lands in Leningrad, and I very much wanted to see that historic city, and the Hermitage.

I had an unforgettable experience on my arrival at the airport in Leningrad. I must explain the background circumstances. I had a Russian friend in Windsor who violently disliked the Soviet regime, and who was a devout member of the Russian Orthodox Church. She suggested to me that, since the Soviet government had closed most of the churches, and no biblical material was available to the ordinary person, I would be doing a good deed by taking some religious tracts (in Russian) into the country and leaving them in a public place. Since she was my very good friend, I agreed to do so, and had these tracts in my briefcase.

On the plane en route to Leningrad there were some American geographers who were also going to the conference, and I told them about the tracts. They said that it was illegal to take religious materials into the Soviet Union, and that I should leave them on the aircraft. Since there had been no seat assignments, I reasoned that on-one could connect these things to me, and pushed them under the seat. I certainly underestimated Soviet officialdom! In the line to go through customs and immigration only a few minutes later, I was surrounded by officials holding the tracts and shouting questions at me in Russian. I'm sure that my face turned scarlet, and I looked very guilty but I kept saying, "I don't understand Russian. I don't know what you are saying." All my friends went on, and I was left alone as the officials searched my luggage. I wondered how I could ask to contact the Canadian Embassy when no-one spoke English, or if I would be sent directly to Siberia (not as a guest of the Soviet Academy of Sciences this time). I admit that I was terrified. After what seemed like hours, I was allowed to go. When

I finally caught up with other conference delegates, they told me that all the Canadians on the plane had also been detained and searched. Perhaps they thought we were some weird religious sect.

As a delegate to the Polar Lands Symposium in Leningrad in
1976, I toured the Soviet research ship 'Professor Viese'

After that unpleasant introduction to Leningrad, I did enjoy the city, and the Polar Lands Symposium which was attended by 100 delegates from the USSR, the USA, Switzerland, Germany, Japan and Canada. We visited an Arctic research ship, and the Institute for Arctic and Antarctic Research, housed in a beautiful palace once owned by a Czarist general. There was time for sightseeing, and high on the list was the Hermitage. I can't imagine a more beautiful art gallery, and it was good to see many school groups also enjoying it. Peter the Great's summer palace was spectacular, as was a trip to Novgorod, the ancient capital of Muscovy, which has been completely restored. We were also allowed to buy tickets to a concert by the famous Kirov Ballet, an unforgettable experience.

I visited the restored ancient city of Novgorod
(now an UNESCO World Heritage Site)

It was then by train to Moscow, the site of the main congress of about 4,000 delegates. The opening ceremonies were most impressive, taking place in the beautiful Palace of Congresses inside the Kremlin. Most of the sessions were held in Moscow University. About 120 papers were given in the Section on Climatology and Hydrology, the Section I attended. I especially remember the session which I chaired. One speaker went on and on, past his allotted time. I asked him to please finish his presentation, but he ignored my request. After a few more minutes, I repeated my request, which was again ignored. I wondered what action to pursue, when a helpful Canadian friend pulled the plug of the projector. I think that was the first and only time I saw that occurrence at a conference. I was invited to receptions at the Canadian Embassy, and the Soviet Academy of Sciences. I was pleased to meet Dr. Davitaya and Dr. Gavrilova again, and thank them for my wonderful visits in 1975. I was not sorry to leave the USSR at the end of the Congress, and fly to London for my connecting flight to Detroit. I found that being an ordinary visitor to the Soviet Union was very different from being an honoured exchange scientist. I have never returned to the Soviet Union or Russia, and never again saw Maria Gavrilova or F.F. Davitaya.

Back in Windsor in the mid 1970s, I found that pollution problems in the Great Lakes were becoming a matter of concern to both Canadians and Americans. Articles in the press stated that Lake Erie was a dead lake. As a result, the International Joint Commission (a joint U.S.-Canada agency formed in 1909 to deal with trans-boundary water problems) requested the governments of Canada and the United States to research the sources of the pollutants. In 1975, a three-year international research effort called PLUARG (Pollution from Land Use Activities Reference Group) was announced. A call for proposals was issued and I forwarded a proposal to study "Precipitation Quantity and Quality in the Canadian Portion of the Lake Erie Watershed." I was very pleased that my proposal was accepted and I was awarded $50,000 by the federal Department of Agriculture. It was my first multi-disciplinary research and I found it interesting working with international scientists from many disciplines.

My work involved the installation of Belfort precipitation gauges (which I had used earlier in Essex County) to measure the monthly amounts of precipitation at six watersheds in southern Ontario. We also used special collectors for water samples to be tested for concentrations of the chemicals of concern: sulphite, nitrogen, phosphate, chloride, calcium, sodium, potassium, magnesium, lead and PCBs. The equipment was installed on six farms, and the samples were collected monthly by one of my graduate students. The chemical tests were done in the chemistry department at the university. We found that many pollutants were entering the lakes by way of precipitation, as well as dry fallout. Our research paper entitled "Surface Loadings from Pollutants in Precipitation in Southern Ontario; some Climatic and Statistical Aspects" was published in the *Journal of Great Lakes Research.*

After my trip to the Soviet Arctic in 1975, I again began thinking of the Canadian Arctic. I had noticed that most of the scientists I met in Yakutsk were local Yakutian people, and I knew that there were few, if any, Inuit scientists in the Canadian north. I discussed with my colleague John Jacobs the idea of giving a university course in Arctic Canada, to try to interest Inuit students in science. John had been doing research in the Baffin Island area for some years, and knew the area well. We agreed that a very worthwhile project would be to give a course called "The Arctic Environment" for students from both northern and southern Canada. In 1976, we persuaded the University of Windsor that such a course should be given. The students would receive a full-course credit for three weeks in the north (realizing that classes would take place for about 10 hours a day for 21 days). We chose Frobisher Bay (now Iqaluit) as the locale, since it was served by a commercial airline, and also had a wonderful building, built by the U.S. Air Force during World War II, where we could stay and hold our classes. With the co-operation of the NWT Department of Education, and financial assistance from a generous Windsor lady, we enrolled 12 Inuit students from the settlements of Frobisher Bay, Igloolik, Cape Dorset, Rankin Inlet, Pangnirtung, Eskimo Point, and Arctic Bay. Twelve students from southern Canada registered – from Windsor, Hamilton, Toronto, Peterborough and Niagara Falls. The course was held in August, 1977. Since John and I were both climatologists, we needed other specialists to make the course truly environmental. We persuaded Paul Hebert from Windsor to teach biology; Giff Miller from Colorado, geology; Phil Howarth from McMaster, geomorphology and remote sensing; and a local Inuit elder, Simonie Alainga, Inuit knowledge of the environment. I was excited to be again going to the Arctic, and especially the eastern Arctic, which I had never seen.

The southern contingent flew from Montreal on First Air, some 2,300 km to Frobisher Bay. Although, as a geographer, I knew that the eastern Arctic would be different from the west, I was still surprised at how different it was. Flying north from Montreal, we soon were beyond farmland, and saw endless miles of trees and rocks and lakes. Most of northern Québec is shield country, with no majestic Mackenzie River.

In mid-July, Ungava Bay and Frobisher Bay were still covered with floating ice. Baffin Island, with its high mountains and glaciers, was very different from the Mackenzie Delta. We finally saw the settlement of Frobisher Bay, named by Martin Frobisher when he explored the area in search of the northwest passage in 1576. The town seemed so small in that vast empty space. About 2,500 people lived there in 1977, while today, as the capital of Nunavut, Iqaluit has more than 7,000 inhabitants. The climate is very different from that in the western Arctic. A warm August day in Iqaluit may record 10°C, not the 20°C which could be expected in Norman Wells at the same latitude. However, the midnight sun was the same, and the students soon became accustomed to being outdoors, even playing baseball, at midnight.

The building where we lived was called "Ukkivik" by the local population (meaning "the place where one spends the winter" in Inuktitut), since many students from other communities did spend the winter there. The huge building was very well built for the northern climate; set on piles, which were frozen into the permafrost. It was quite luxurious, with comfortable bedrooms, bathrooms with running water, cafeteria, classrooms, and even a bowling alley. The U.S. Air Force had constructed the building and the runway, and had spared no expense. We slept, ate and had classes in "Ukkivik." It was perfect for our course.

We had a very busy schedule. Usually the mornings were spent in the classroom, and the afternoons out-of-doors. John Jacobs began the lectures with a definition of "Arctic," and also did the meteorology lectures. I did the lectures in climatology and hydrology, and our visiting lecturers spoke of geology, the plants and animals of the Arctic, and the peoples who inhabited this part of the world. Our Inuit instructor, Simonie Alainga, told the students of the local Inuit culture, and gave lessons in the Inuktitut language. In the afternoons, the students did pace-and-compass surveys, used the radiation equipment to determine the energy balances of various surfaces, and with Paul Hebert became acquainted with the local interesting plants and flowers. With Phil Howarth, we hiked on the tundra outside the town, and looked at the geological formations and various periglacial landforms. We dug beneath the surface to actually touch the permafrost. This impressed the southern students, but not the northerners, who said, "We walk on the surface of the land. We don't care what's underneath." We visited the weather station at the airport and watched a weather balloon launch. We visited a hydrometric station, where the flow of the Sylvia Grinnell River was measured.

A Baffin Island inukshuk. These man-made structures
are striking features in the treeless tundra

A highlight of the course was a five-day camping trip down the bay to Ward Inlet. We organized a fishing boat to take all 28 of us to our campsite, a favourite one for the local Inuit, where we pitched our tents, a difficult task for some of the southerners. We took turns cooking over an open fire. We had to deal with the reality of no bathrooms. The students built inukshuks of the local rocks (the word "inukshuk" means "like a man" in the Inuktitut language). There were many inukshuks in the area, as directional aids in a landscape in which it is easy to lose direction.

During our stay in Frobisher Bay, we learned a lot about the community. We visited the local museum, located in the former liquor store. (Alcohol could not be purchased in Frobisher Bay.) However, there was one hotel, the Frobisher Inn, where we could go in the evenings for a beer. We were informed that there was a bouncer who would evict anyone who appeared to be inebriated. In the harbour, we watched the government supply ships unloading their cargoes in a most unusual fashion. Since there is a very large tidal range in Frobisher Bay, the ships sailed up the bay on a high tide, so when the tide went out, they were on dry land and could be easily unloaded. We had a tour of the "Calanus," a veteran Arctic oceanographic vessel which was in the harbour for repairs, and invited the captain for dinner at Ukkivik. On Sundays, some of us went to the lovely igloo-shaped Anglican Church, where the hymns and sermon were in Inuktitut, and the kneelers were made of sealskin. We were very impressed with the local schools, but saddened to hear that very few of the Inuit students finished high school. One aspect of the landscape that all of us will remember, was the prevalence of empty oil drums. Of course, oil has to be brought from the south to supply the need for power, but we were told that it was too expensive to ship the empty drums south again. Other obvious features of the treeless landscape were the utilidors. Because of the permafrost, the pipes carrying water and sewage are about two feet above ground, and insulated against the freezing temperatures. As in all northern communities, there is a Hudson Bay store, where one could buy just about everything, and also the local craft shop where Inuit carvings are for sale.

I think the course was successful. Certainly, the southern students found the Arctic fascinating, and I hope that the Inuit students learned a little science. I remember especially two of the Inuit students. Anne Meekitjuk Hanson was a beautiful woman who had, as a teenager, played the leading female role in the movie *The White Dawn*, a Hollywood movie based on the book of the same name by James Houston. She had three lovely daughters who went on our camping trip with us. She was, without doubt, our best student, and went on to do great things for Iqaluit and the Inuit people. She was invited to Ottawa to dine with the Queen on one of her visits to Canada. Anne has also been honoured with the Order of Canada for her work with native people and the CBC. I also remember Peter Ittinuar from Rankin Inlet, who became the first Inuk to be elected to the House of Commons.

When we flew south at the end of the course, I knew that I would like to return to this interesting area. In Windsor that fall, John and Paul and I decided to make the course an annual event. We repeated the course in Frobisher in 1978 and 1979, and each year was different.

Paul and John and I were the regular instructors, and we usually invited other Arctic specialists to supplement the curriculum. We also did different field trips. I will never forget the trip in 1978. We flew in a charter aircraft to Pangnirtung, north of Frobisher Bay, a beautiful village formerly used by whalers, and now the gateway to spectacular Auyuittuq Park. Before landing at 'Pang' the pilot flew up the fiord-like Pangnirtung Pass, and then turned the plane sideways, so we were looking into the face of the glacier. I think that not many people have seen a glacier from that angle! To our surprise, he then landed the plane, although there was no runway. We were all a little terrified, but it was an unforgettable, and probably illegal, look at Auyuittuq Park. We camped near the picturesque village of Pangnirtung, visited the Hudson Bay store, and the weaving shop, and on Sunday attended the local Anglican Church, where the service was in the Inuktitut language.

Our plane actually landed in Auyuittuq Park
near Pangnirtung in Baffin Island

In 1980, we decided to hold the course in Igloolik, a settlement on Igloolik Island to the northwest of Frobisher in the Foxe Basin. We chose Igloolik because of its unique research station, a circular building on stilts that certainly dominated the hamlet. Here there was no Ukkivik, and we lived in a rented house and made our own meals. The students and staff took turns cooking, visiting the local hunters and trappers' store to buy Arctic char and caribou. There was no running water in our house (water was delivered by truck about twice a week), and the students were at first a little skeptical of the "honey bucket" in the bathroom. The research station was an ideal place for lectures, with its good library and 360 degree views. For our field trip, we chartered an aircraft for the flight to Hall Beach on the mainland of Keewatin, where we camped at an abandoned DEW Line site.

We chose the hamlet of Igloolik on Igloolik Island in the Foxe Basin, Nunavut, as the site for our Arctic Environment course in 1980

The Igloolik Research Centre was ideal for lectures and research

I remember vividly the return trip to southern Canada. I found out that First Air flew from Igloolik to Repulse Bay on the western shore of Hudson Bay, and from there to Churchill where we could connect with a flight to Windsor. I persuaded several of our students to return home by this route to see a new landscape. Of course in the north, flights always depend on the weather, and we landed in Repulse Bay to find that poor weather prevented our take-off for Churchill. We were stranded in Repulse Bay for two days. There was no hotel, but we were allowed to stay at a construction site for a very substantial fee, and make our own meals. I was the only female, so I agreed to make the dinners, if my companions would forgo television and converse at the table.

In 1981, we were in Frobisher again, but that was our last University of Windsor Arctic course. Each year the airfare became more expensive, and after the first year in 1977, we had not been successful in attracting Inuit students, so our courses had comprised only southern students. John and Paul and I realized that our goal of interesting Inuit students in science had not been a success, although I think our course was the first university-credit course given in the Arctic.

There are dates in one's life that can never be forgotten. One such date for me was October 10, 1978, when Bob went for a walk after dinner as he often did. He never took identification or his wallet on these walks. Two hours went by and he hadn't returned. I thought he may have gone to visit a friend, but feared the worst when a policeman came to the door, and asked to see my husband. When I said that Bob had gone for a walk and hadn't returned, the policeman suggested that he might be in the hospital, and asked me to go there with him. He didn't tell me that Bob had collapsed on the street with a massive heart attack, and had died instantly. A teenage bystander evidently told the policeman that he knew where the man lived, and brought him to our house.

I couldn't believe that Bob was dead. He had had minor heart attacks before, but he had always recovered. He loved life, especially because he had so narrowly escaped death during the war. He was a wonderful husband and father. He seemed very young; he had just celebrated his 58th birthday.

I had the sad task of phoning our children, and they came home immediately. They helped me with all the funeral arrangements. The memorial service for Bob was held in Chalmers United Church, where we had been members since moving to Willistead Crescent. A great many people came to the service, since Bob was a very popular member of the community, and loved by his patients. He was buried in the family plot in the cemetery in Chesley.

CHAPTER 6
Hawaii, the Arctic and the Great Lakes Institute

I found that life went on after Bob's death, and I was fortunate to have a job to keep me busy. Jimmy decided to come home to live with me, and take the Geology program at the University of Windsor, so I wasn't lonely. And in January 1979, I received a letter that gave me a new interest in life. It was an invitation from Roland Fuchs, head of the Department of Geography at the University of Hawaii in Honolulu, to be a visiting professor in the fall term of 1979. It was just what I needed to recover from Bob's death. I accepted immediately, especially as I was due for a sabbatical leave in 1979-1980, and had made no other plans. I looked forward very much to living in Hawaii, which I heard was very beautiful, and which I had never visited. I also looked forward to teaching at a large university with a big geography department and a PhD program. I had never had doctoral students before. I was asked to teach a second-year climatology class, and a seminar course for graduate climatology students. Another stroke of good luck was that one of the professors, Lyndon Wester, was on leave, and rented me his beautiful apartment right on the ocean at Kapiolani Park near Diamond Head.

I flew to Honolulu in late August. I was met at the airport by two of the graduate students, Tom Giambelluca and Yasuo Noguchi, who presented me with a beautiful lei. (I was to find that it was customary to meet visitors to the Islands with a lei.) I fell in love with Hawaii immediately; the apartment, the climate, the flowers, and the ocean. I woke to the sound of the surf, and ate breakfast on my balcony (called a lanai in Hawaii), overlooking the ocean. Five days a week I walked across Kapiolani Park to take the bus to the university in the Manoa valley, about a 20-minute ride from downtown Honolulu. Roland Fuchs introduced me to the other members of the department (all men) who were very friendly. I especially remember Donald Fryer, originally from England, who lectured on the Geography of Europe and the History of Geographic Thought. He was familiar with Griffith Taylor's name and we had great discussions about the history of geography. I also remember how helpful the two beautiful Hawaiian secretaries were. I found that present-day Hawaiians, who are descendants of the original Polynesians, intermarried with Japanese, Chinese and Caucasians immigrants, are very attractive people.

My climatology students at the University of Hawaii
visited the weather station at the Honolulu airport

I enjoyed the university, and my students genuinely appeared to like climatology, and to like me. For my second-year course I used the same syllabus as I had in Windsor, based on the radiation, energy and water balances. Since no general text on the Hawaiian climate was available, I spent a great deal of time searching for Hawaiian data to illustrate my lectures. I had taken my Windsor radiation equipment with me and found that the students loved doing actual research on the radiation balances of various surfaces. I managed to arrange a trip to the airport weather station, near Pearl Harbor, to show them how weather observations were made. Because of its volcanic soils and no surface water, water supply is a problem in Hawaii, so I spent a good deal of time on the water balance with my graduate students. Several of the research papers they did that fall were very good, and were published in refereed journals. They were a most impressive group of students (all male) from many different countries.

I read all I could find about Hawaii. The state is composed of eight main islands, none of them very large, lying just inside the tropics. The largest is Hawaii (called the Big Island), about 4,000 square miles in area, and the smallest, Kahoolawe, is only 45 square miles. Maui is the second largest, and with Oahu, is the most popular for tourists. The capital, Honolulu, is on Oahu. The islands are quite young geologically, with Kauai in the northwest the oldest (about 5 million years old), and the Big Island in the southeast the youngest. (With its active volcanoes and lava flows, it is still growing.) The Big Island has two massive shield volcanoes, Mauna Kea and Mauna Loa, with summits more than 13,000 feet above sea level. Because of their position in the zone of the northeast trade winds, and because of the mountainous topography, the Islands have many different climates; tropical rain forests, grasslands, deserts – even tundra areas. They resemble continents in miniature. Because of their position in the middle of the vast Pacific Ocean and just inside the tropics, the Hawaiian Islands enjoy moderate temperatures year-round; never too hot and never too cool.

Since distances between the islands are not large, and airfares were cheap, I often visited other islands on the weekends. Early in the fall, I flew to the Big Island to see Mauna Loa, the large mountain that has near its summit an observatory measuring atmospheric compounds. At this time (1979) the world was first hearing about global warming, and the possible role played by atmospheric CO2, so I was very interested in visiting the Mauna Loa Observatory. Jim Juvik, a geographer at the University of Hawaii at Hilo, obtained permission for us to drive from Hilo to the Observatory 11,200 ft. above sea level. It was a spectacular drive from the lush forests at Hilo to tundra vegetation, and then bare black lava near the summit. It was fascinating to talk to the scientists at the Observatory, and to see the complicated equipment. It was also, for me, a nauseating experience, since one's body has trouble adjusting to a large change in altitude in a few hours. I found that I had trouble breathing, and I'm afraid that I was walking very unsteadily. After a few hours at this very high altitude, it was a relief to drive to a lower elevation and be taken to my hotel. However, nature had another surprise for me. During the night, I was awakened by my bed shaking and pictures falling off the walls. I realized that an earthquake was occurring, but I felt too ill to leave my room, and I stayed in bed. In the morning, I was told that the earthquake measured 6.4 on the Richter scale!

On another weekend, I visited the Volcanoes National Park on the Big Island, where I saw recent lava flows, and actually felt the ground hot under my feet. Kauai, called the "garden island" was another weekend visit, as was Molokai, the site of a former leper colony. I went twice to Maui. Its large mountain, Haleakala, with its enormous 3,000 ft. deep crater, was thought by the early Hawaiians to be the home of the sun. It is spectacular to see the sunrise over Haleakala.

Of course, I got to know Oahu very well. I learned early that one bus ticket would enable me to travel all around the island, so I often took advantage of this bargain. A favourite destination was the North Shore, world-famous for its surfing beaches. At Sunset Beach, the waves were so huge that I didn't even step into the water. I found that agriculture in Oahu was mostly pineapple production, and the Dole pineapple fields in the interior of the island were enormous. A good deal of sugar cane was also grown. There are several large military establishments on Oahu including, of course, the huge naval base at Pearl Harbor. I think every visitor to Oahu visits the Arizona Memorial at Pearl Harbor and I was no exception. It was a very moving experience.

The waves are huge at Sunset Beach on the north shore of Oahu

There were many things to do on weekends. I like swimming, and the ocean was always a perfect temperature. I spent a lot of time at Sans Souci Beach (loved by Mark Twain), only a few steps from my apartment. There was a Kodak Hula Show in Kapiolani Park, and also hula shows at many of the big hotels in Waikiki. The hula dances illustrate the history of Hawaii, and are a very special part of the culture. Another very interesting destination was the Polynesian Cultural Center, several hours north of Honolulu. A project of the Church of Latter Day Saints, the Center contains actual villages in a beautiful tropical setting from many Polynesian cultures: Fiji, Tonga, Tahiti, the Marquesas and New Zealand. Brigham Young University brings students from these islands to take part in the production, but they also take classes and receive a university education.

The Polynesian Cultural Center beautifully portrays
many cultures of the South Pacific Islands

In Honolulu, it was common to hear people speaking the Hawaiian language. It sounds very soft, since there are very few consonants, and every letter is pronounced (for example, the word for rainbow "anuenue" is pronounced "a-noo-ee-noo-ee"). There are also some peculiarities to confuse the newcomer in Oahu. One is directions. No-one uses the words north, east, south, etc. Toward the ocean is "moana"; toward the mountains "mauka"; northeast is "Diamond Head" and southwest is "Ewa." Visitors are called 'haoles."

It is believed that the first settlers in Hawaii were Polynesians, who managed to reach the Islands from Fiji, and families who have Polynesian blood have high status in Hawaii. The missionaries arrived in the 18th century, and it is often said, "They came to do good, and they did very well for themselves." (Many of the large businesses are controlled by descendants of the missionary families.) It seemed to me that the population is still very religious. There are many churches and many denominations. I often went to the Kawaiahao church, built about 1840, originally the chapel of the Hawaian royal family, now called the Westminster Abbey of Hawaii. It is a lovely church, where the hymns were sung in the Hawaiian language, and the elders were

large Hawaiian ladies, very impressive in their elegant muumuus. The missionaries had introduced the very comfortable muumuus to the Islands.

With my classes and my exploration of Oahu and the other islands, I found that the semester passed all too quickly, and in mid-December it was time to return to Canada. I realized that I had found another favourite place in the world. I agreed with Mark Twain when he wrote that the Hawaiian Islands were "the loveliest fleet of islands that lies anchored in any ocean."

Since I was still on sabbatical after Christmas, I accepted an invitation from Environment Canada to be a delegate to a World Climate Conference in Geneva in Switzerland in January, 1980. This was the beginning of the world-wide interest in climate change, and as a climatologist, I wanted to attend. It was my first visit to that lovely city, and I enjoyed the conference, held at the Headquarters of the World Meteorological Organization. I also loved to ski, so I took the opportunity to stay in Switzerland after the conference, to ski for a week in Zermatt, at the base of the Matterhorn, one of the most beautiful of the Alpine ski villages. No cars are allowed in the village, so one must walk or take a horse-drawn carriage. I joined a ski class, and met interesting people. I also liked the cog railway that took skiers to the top of the mountain. I didn't need to contend with rope tows or T-bars, as in Filzmoos. Sometimes one run would take all day. I decided that I liked skiing in the Alps.

Ever since becoming a professor of geography, I had maintained a membership in the Canadian Association of Geographers, and I usually managed to attend the annual conferences. Since they were held at various universities across Canada, it was a great way to see Canada. In 1972, I was elected a councillor of the CAG, and in 1979 Vice-President. It was quite an honour in 1980 to be elected President, the first female president of the organization founded in 1951. I was lucky to be President that year, since the IGU (which meets every four years) was held in Tokyo, and I attended as a member of the official Canadian delegation.

This was my first trip to the Far East, and I enjoyed Japan. I remember especially the crowds of people, the traffic, the signs which I couldn't read, and also the lovely oasis of the Otani hotel, where I stayed. It was one of the most beautiful hotels I have visited. The flower arrangements were spectacular, the room beautiful, and the food was delicious. I remember one breakfast when I was served an orange, cut and arranged like a flower. I actually took a course in flower arranging, one of the offerings at the conference. I don't recall much about the meetings, except that, as part of the "History of Geographical Thought" program, I spent three days in Kyoto, a lovely city filled with beautiful temples. I travelled there on the "Bullet Train" at, I think, more than 200 miles an hour.

In 1980, since I was still on sabbatical leave, I decided to begin a new project; writing a biography of my early mentor at UofT, Griffith Taylor. I had always remembered him with great affection, and kept in touch with him after he returned to Australia in 1951, until his death in 1963. I wrote to Bill Taylor, Grif's son, who lived in Sydney, to tell him about my project and asked if I could come to interview him in the summer of 1980. He put me in touch with two of his father's students: Sister Nell Stanley, a teacher at Holy Cross Convent in Sydney, and Brock Rowe, who at 76 was still very active in geographical affairs in Australia.

My visit to Australia started off badly. I arranged to have a stop over in Honolulu to visit my friends at the university, and had a lovely three days there. However, when I was checking in for the flight to Sydney, I was asked for my visa for Australia. This surprised me and I answered "I don't need a visa, I am a Canadian citizen." To this, the reply was, "I don't care who you are, lady, you can't get on this plane without a visa." I was appalled, since my travel agent had never told me that I needed a visa for Australia. I returned to my hotel in Honolulu, and spent a busy few days obtaining a visa. I found that I needed my police record. I phoned my neighbour in Windsor, Mark MacGuigan (Canada's Minister of External Affairs at the time), who kindly expedited the visa for me.

I found Sydney to be a beautiful city, and understood why Taylor liked it so much. Brock Rowe loved telling me his recollections of Grif, as did Sister Nell Stanley, who invited me for lunch in her convent (my first and only visit to a convent). Bill Taylor was most gracious and invited me for dinner to talk about his father. He astounded me by giving me his father's personals diaries. Grif had kept a diary from the age of 16 until his death, and these personal accounts were invaluable to me in the writing of the biography. Several years later, I took the diaries to the Scott Polar Research Institute in Cambridge, England, where they will remain in perpetuity.

I visited the University of Sydney, where some of the professors remembered Taylor, but I found that there was little Taylor material in the Geography archives. Grif had requested that most of his papers and books be given to the National Archives in Canberra, so I spent a week in that city. I don't remember much about Canberra, since I spent the greatest part of every day in the Archives. I found that there were 30 feet of Taylor material, very well organized into 13 series from "Early Years" (1880-1910) to "Retirement" (1951-1963). There was a box of his medals. The most interesting was the Antarctic Polar Medal (silver) given to Taylor by King George V in 1914, and the David Livingstone Centenary Medal (gold) given to him by the American Geographical Society in 1923. The number of books and articles produced by Taylor during his lifetime was truly amazing.

After my busy time in Australia, I felt that I should have a holiday, and spent a week in New Zealand visiting and sight-seeing. Warren Moran was a professor of geography at the University of Auckland, and a friend of my sister Joan and her husband Quentin, both U of T geography graduates. Warren and his wife invited me to visit them in their lovely home in Auckland, and I spent a day at the university. I had a one-day trip to the south, to Rotorua, where the lava fields reminded me of the volcanic landscapes in Hawaii.

In the fall of 1980, my friend Paul Hebert and I discussed the possibility of forming a Great Lakes Institute at the University of Windsor. I had been a member of IAGLR (International Association of Great Lakes Research) since my PhD student days, and had attended the annual meetings. We knew that there had been a Great Lakes Institute at the University of Toronto for many years, but it had changed into an Institute for Environmental Studies. Paul and I felt that there should be a research facility at a Canadian university, as there were at many American universities, devoted solely to Great Lakes studies. We were successful in having our proposal for a Great Lakes Institute at the University of Windsor approved by the university administration, and I felt honoured to be appointed the first director of this fledgling Institute.

We wished the Institute to be multi-disciplinary, and were successful in obtaining members from such diverse departments as geology, engineering, biology, economics, political science and law. It was interesting that only one female professor, Maxine Holder-Franklin of Biology, requested membership. We were also successful in obtaining a very good Advisory Board composed of influential government scientists, among them Art Collin, Jim Bruce and Walter Giles.

With the help of our government advisors, we decided that our first area of research should be one of considerable public concern, pollution in the Great Lakes, and we put together a large proposal entitled "A Case Study of Selected Toxic Contaminants in the Essex Region." Our proposal involved 10 research groups, from the departments of geography, biology, economics, geology, political science and law. The contaminants selected were lead, cadmium, PCBs and octachlorostyrene, considered to be the most serious environmental contaminants. In 1982, Environment Canada awarded us a very large grant of $800,000. (For those not familiar with university research grants, I should explain how research money is used. In the case of our Environment Canada grant, there were 10 research groups who needed funds for equipment, for the chemical tests, and for student stipends. Many graduate students are supported by research grants. None of the money goes to the professors, who oversee the work and quite often write the final reports.)

My part of the research was the testing of precipitation for the four contaminants at various locations in Essex County. This followed logically from our earlier work in precipitation chemistry. It was not surprising to find that rain and snow in Essex County were not pure water, but contained significant quantities of all the pollutants. Our research findings were published in 1985 in the *Journal of Great Lakes Research* with the title "Surface Loading of Lead and Cadmium from Precipitation in Essex County." The biologists on our team, under Paul Hebert's guidance, focused on the aquatic species in the Detroit River, Lake St. Clair, and the St. Clair River. There are many chemical companies lining the St. Clair River near Sarnia, and the biologists found only dead clams in that area. The *Windsor Star* newspaper reported the findings, which were then trumpeted in the national press as "The St. Clair River Blob." I am quite sure that our research was instrumental in causing the chemical companies to clean up their discharges into the St. Clair River.

The early 1980s were enjoyable years for me. My three geography lecture courses, plus my Great Lakes Institute research kept me busy, while I used any spare time to begin writing my biography of Griffith Taylor. I decided that I should visit Cambridge and the Scott Polar Research Institute (SPRI) to see the material they had on Taylor. Harry King, the Institute librarian was most helpful to me. I had copies made of several of Ponting's photos of Grif. (Herbert Ponting was the official photographer on the expedition and produced some thousand negatives during his time in the Antarctic. These historic negatives are now in the possession of the SPRI.) I heard that Captain Scott's son, Sir Peter Scott, was then living near Oxford and he kindly agreed to see me. I had tea with him at his home in Slimbridge, and we talked about his father and the Antarctic Expedition. Although he knew Taylor's name, he said that he had never met the man. However, for me it was a thrill to meet and speak to a person connected with the Scott Antarctic Expedition.

In 1983, I again went skiing in Europe, this time to a little place in the French Alps called Flaine. I had read about Flaine in an English newspaper while I was in England. It was not far from Geneva in the Haute-Savoie area, noted for its large amounts of snow. I flew to Geneva and rented a car to drive to Flaine, and stayed in a hotel for a week. I joined a ski class and found that the "pistes" were not too difficult for me. It was a lovely area in the shadow of Mont Blanc. The development was like Zermatt, with no cars allowed, and it was only a short walk to the gondola that took me to the top of the mountain. Before my week's holiday was over, I decided to buy a condominium in Flaine. My children thought it was an impulsive gesture and wondered at my sanity, but we all enjoyed the skiing there for the five years that I owned the condo.

I usually managed a winter and a summer holiday, flying to Geneva and renting a car for the two-hour trip to Flaine. The last part of the drive, with hairpin turns, was rather scary, especially after a big snow storm. Quite often, when my holiday ended, I found my car completely buried in snow. I had found an agent, Nicholas, who rented the condo for me when I wasn't using it. This seemed like a good idea, until one winter my my son Hardie and daughter-in-law Leslie arrived at the condo to find it already occupied. Obviously, Nicholas had been renting it at times without telling me. (As a friend of mine said "He'd be a fool not to!") Sometimes I holidayed alone, and sometimes some of my family or friends joined me. I especially remember one Christmas Eve with soft snow falling, no cars and no noise, and skiers coming down the mountain with lighted torches. It was magical! Summers were pleasant too with hiking in the mountains, and trips to Provence and the Mediterranean. Although I enjoyed Flaine, and the skiing, I decided to sell the condo in 1988. I realized that being an absentee landlord wasn't a very good idea.

I loved my life at the university with my classes and the Great Lakes Institute, and quite often a new challenge. In the mid-1980s I received an interesting invitation was to be a member of UNESCO's International Hydrological Program, whose meetings were held twice a year in Paris. I was asked to be the editor of an English source book in climatology for hydrologists and water resource engineers. Four Soviet climatologists worked with me on the book: Drs. Markova, Kuznetsova, Borzenkova and Budyko (only Olga Markova attended the meetings). Dr. Markova and I wrote the Introduction; Dennis Nullet, my student at the University of Hawaii wrote about the Radiation and Energy Balances, and my friend Russ Mather wrote the chapter The Water Balance of the Earth's Surface. The other chapters were written by the Soviet climatologists and it was necessary for me, as editor, to rewrite much of the English. However, the chapter entitled "Future Climatic Change" written by Soviet climatologist M. Budyko (whom I had never succeeded in meeting when I was in the USSR in 1975) was very well-written and did not require any editing. It is interesting to read today (2009) Budyko's concluding statement: "The above conclusions about the low probability of disastrous consequences of climatic change may change the insufficiently substantiated suggestions of a number of politicians on this question." The book, entitled *UNESCO Sourcebook in Climatology for Hydrologists and Water Resource Engineers* was published in 1990.

Most of my time after lectures was spent on Great Lakes Institute affairs. After the completion of the toxic contaminant research, we began to work on another proposal in the mid-1980s. Climate change was becoming much talked about, and our Advisory Board suggested that government funding was available for research on the impact of global warming on navigation and hydro-power development in the Great Lakes. We put together a research team and sent the proposal to Environment Canada's Atmospheric Environment Service for a study entitled "Implications of Climate Change for Navigation and Power Development in the Great Lakes."

We were awarded $90,000 for the three year study. Our four teams of researchers from the Departments of Geography, Economics, Political Science and Faculty of Law used the scenarios of climate change and future lake levels obtained from the Canada Centre for Inland Waters in Burlington. Our report to Environment Canada was published in their "Climate Change Digest 87-03" and was much quoted. A summary of the navigation aspect, written by my student Darrell Marchand and myself, was submitted to the journal *Climatic Change* and published in that journal in 1988 with the title "Climatic Change and Great Lakes Levels: the Impact on Shipping." Our study concluded, "If climate change occurs, coupled with increased consumptive use of Great Lakes water, the frequency of low lake levels such as those experienced during the mid-1960s could occur much more frequently." Our socio-economic model, relating lake levels to shipping costs, indicated that, with climate change, the average costs for Great Lakes shipping companies would increase by 30%.

In 1986, I was again asked by Roland Fuchs at the University of Hawaii to be a visiting lecturer in geography in the winter term of 1987 and, of course, I eagerly accepted. I had found no place on earth more beautiful than Hawaii! Again I found an apartment on the ocean near Diamond Head. It was great to be back at the university, and for the first time in my teaching career, I had a female colleague, Nancy Davis. I again taught a graduate and an undergraduate course in climatology, and was most impressed with the graduate students. There were even some female graduate students.

During my earlier term in Hawaii, I had met several professors in departments other than geography, who lectured on aspects of the Hawaiian climate. I decided to approach them with the idea of writing a book on Hawaiian climate, since I had never found one on the topic. I was pleased to find five scientists interested in participating. Tom Schroeder in the Department of Meteorology agreed to write about meteorology; my student, Dennis Nullet, the radiation and energy balances; Tom Giambelucca (then a doctoral student), water in Hawaii; Saul Price, retired from the National Weather Service Forecast Office in Hawaii, impacts on humans; Paul Ekern, from the Water Resources Research Center, climate and agriculture. We started on the book that winter, but after I returned to Canada, we had to correspond by mail – there was no e-mail then! I managed a few trips to Honolulu in the next few years to meet with the authors and the University of Hawaii Press, who had agreed to publish the book. It took longer than we thought to complete. It was finally published in 1993.

I must mention an unusual event that winter of 1987. I was in my office at the university when the secretary excitedly told me that there was a tsunami warning for Honolulu, and that I should return home immediately. (I had been told of the occurrence of tsunamis in Hawaii, especially the one in 1960 that struck Hilo in the Big Island. Many hundreds of people were swept out to sea when they had gone to the seashore to observe the phenomenon.) My sister Gwen was visiting me at the time, and I was worried that she wouldn't know what to do when she heard the loudspeakers trumpeting "This is a tsunami warning. Go to higher ground." I immediately took the bus to Waikiki, where I was saw something most unusual – all the stores were boarded up and the streets were deserted. From there I ran to my apartment which was on the ground floor, but Gwen was nowhere to be seen. Some people were standing on the roof terrace looking at the ocean, so I joined them. It was probably not a smart thing to do, but I reasoned that about two hours had passed since the warning, and perhaps there would not be a tsunami. But where was my sister? A few hours later, she arrived in a car with a young Japanese couple. She had quite a story to tell. She had heard the announcement and reasoned that the nearest "higher ground" would be the slopes of Diamond Head. She ran up the mountain, through peoples' backyards, until the Japanese couple rescued her, and took her into their home for tea. When the "All Clear" sounded they had driven her to my apartment, all of this without a word of English being spoken. How typical this was of the friendly Hawaiian "Aloha Spirit."

I have written earlier about Chinese graduate student Chun-fen Lee whom I had met at UofT in the 1940s. I knew that he had returned to

China and had become a professor of geography. My friend Don Kerr (in Toronto) and I were amazed to hear from him in 1975. He wrote that he would be visiting the United States, and asked Don and me to meet him at the Renaissance Center in Detroit. Don came to Windsor, and we took a bus to Detroit. We were not sure how Chun-fen would look, and how he had survived the Cultural Revolution. We were very surprised to see him in an elegant black coat with a fur collar. He told us that he had taught at the prestigious East China Normal University in Shanghai, and that he, and his family, had suffered a good deal during the Revolution. The university had been closed, and Chun-fen was forced to be a street cleaner. However, he had survived and had been re-instated at the university as a senior professor.

After our visit, I corresponded with Chun-fen. In 1986, he suggested that I apply for a SSHRC (Social Sciences and Humanities Research Council of Canada) Bilateral Exchange Award with the People's Republic of China. It was necessary that I have invitations from three academic institutions in China. With Chun-fen's help, I was invited to the Department of Geography at the East China Normal University, the Nanjing Institute of Hydrology and Water Resources, and the Institute of Geography, Chinese Academy of Sciences, in Beijing. I received the award, and left for China in June, 1987 for a three week visit to the People's Republic of China.

The flight from Vancouver was 12 hours long. We flew up the coast of Alaska and down the east coast of Japan to Shanghai. I had wondered what the Chinese landscape would look like, and, as we came in to land, I was astonished at the greenness of the countryside, with lots of rivers, canals and flooded rice fields – water everywhere. I was met by Miss Zhao, my guide and interpreter in Shanghai, and Professor Tang from the Department of Geography of Shanghai's East China Normal University. As I found everywhere in China, we had a car and driver, usually a young woman who always wore white gloves. I was taken to the university's guest house (a rather shabby cement building) to my room on the third floor. It was certainly Spartan, with a single bed, no sheets or pillowcase, one towel (very small), and the bathroom down the hall. The cafeteria for foreign guests was across the street, and I had breakfasts there (quite a Western breakfast with toast and eggs) and, of course, tea. Professor Tang told me that unfortunately, Chun-fen Lee was in hospital and couldn't welcome me, but that I would visit him later.

My first visit was to the Department of Geography to meet the staff and students. In front of the building was a large sign stating, "Welcome Professor Marie Sanderson." I was certainly treated with the utmost respect and friendliness, no doubt because I was a friend of the beloved Professor Lee! There were 50 professors in the department and six PhD students, all of whom spoke very good English. I gave three lectures in the next few days. As in the USSR, a lecture took a lot of time, since I had to stop at the end of each sentence so the translation could be given. The students asked very good questions. A few of them asked me to exchange some Chinese currency for American dollars which they needed to apply for study at a Canadian university. Of course I did, only to discover that I couldn't use the Chinese currency, even for a taxi. At that time (1987), the only stores where tourists could shop were the "Friendship Stores," and they were full of interesting things for which one needed hard currency.

In Shanghai I visited my friend Chun-fen Lee, a professor
at the East China Normal University, and the recipient
of the first Geography PhD degree in Canada

One day, Dr. Lee's daughter took me to see Chun-fen. He was in a very VIP hospital, more like a hotel than a hospital, certainly not what I had expected. We had a great chat, remembering our friendship of 40 years and our mutual respect for Griffith Taylor. He told me that he had inaugurated geography as a university discipline in China, and had brought Taylor's philosophy of geography to China. He loved to talk about Toronto and his happy memories of UofT. It was an emotional visit and the last time I would see my old friend. We continued our correspondence for many years, and I was sad to hear of his death in 1996.

I was taken on many trips around Shanghai. One was a boat trip on the Huang Po River on a very VIP boat, with luxurious appointments and delicious food, even a magic act. I was also taken to visit Chun-fen's wife and daughter at their "private" house. It was a detached house, but not very private, as nine people lived there: two sons and daughters-in-law, and three grandchildren, as well as the Lees. On my last night, the vice-president of the university gave a banquet in my honour. After my very busy week in Shanghai, I was taken to the railway station by Miss Zhao and Professor Tang, in the departmental car with the driver in her white gloves. It was a four-hour trip to Nanjing, and I could not have imagined the density of the population in the "rural" area between these two large cities.

In Nanjing, my guest house was the former British Consulate, so my room was much more luxurious than the one in Shanghai, with a private bath and even air-conditioning. My host was Pu Peimin, the Director of the Institute of Hydrology and Water Resources, a small dynamo of a man who spoke excellent English. He had attended IAGLR meetings in the United States, and knew friends of mine at the University of Michigan. He was eager to establish research connections with our Great Lakes Institute. I gave two lectures in Nanjing on our Great Lakes Institute research. I went on tours of the city and countryside. I was very impressed to see the great Yangtze River and the monument to Sun Yat Sen. There were thousands of Chinese tourists at the monument, climbing the 400 steps to the mausoleum.

After a week in Nanjing, I was taken to the airport by Pu and several colleagues. I was the only non-Chinese in the waiting room. Passengers walked out on the tarmac to board the rather small plane for Beijing.

I found that the landscape around Beijing was very different from that around Shanghai, with brown rather than green the predominant colour. I was met at the airport by Mr. Mu from the Institute of Geography, who drove me to my air-conditioned hotel room with again a private bathroom (although I was becoming accustomed to the bathrooms at the universities, with holes in the floors for toilets and no toilet paper).

On my first day in Beijing, I was taken on a trip to the Great Wall. We left at 7:00 a.m. for the two-hour trip with the driver in her white gloves (this time with a boy-friend for company). Unfortunately it was pouring rain when we arrived, and there seemed to be hundreds of tour buses discharging their passengers to walk along the wall. I was not prepared for the size of the Great Wall. It disappeared into the distance in both directions, but it was so wide that chariots or groups of people could walk abreast. I found that it was all steeply up or steeply down, so I walked only to the first tower – in the rain. Then it was on to the Ming tombs, again massive and impressive. I think that our driver was pleased when we stopped near the Ming tombs for a lovely lunch. (Lunch usually meant about six or more courses!) That night I was taken to the Peking Opera, and the next day to the Summer Palace and the Forbidden City. The Summer Palace is in a beautiful park by a lake, and is a cool and pleasant place to visit. The Forbidden City is certainly impressive with 9,000 rooms in the many palaces. The courtyards, the open spaces, everything is on such a massive scale, all surrounded by a wall and moat.

On my first day in Beijing, I was taken to the Great
Wall of China. I walked only to the first tower

The official part of my visit was fine. I was growing accustomed
to speaking slowly and waiting for the interpretation of each sentence.
I gave two lectures in Beijing, one at the Institute of Geography and
one at Peking University. I enjoyed the city, and even went for early
morning walks on my own, always astonished at the amazing variety
of things that can be carried on bicycles. In 1987 there were millions of
bicycles, but few cars. I must confess that, after three weeks in China
with non-stop activities, I was not sorry to say good-bye to my Beijing
hosts. I took a Japan Airlines flight to Honolulu where I relaxed, and
visited the university to consult with my co-authors of the Hawaiian
climate book.

Almost anything can be carried by bicycle in Beijing

Back in Windsor, I was very pleased to receive a letter from Carleton University Press stating that they would publish my biography of Griffith Taylor in 1988. The editor, David Knight, suggested the title *Griffith Taylor: Antarctic Scientist and Pioneer Geographer*. The cover of the paperback edition showed a sketch of Taylor done by Bill Wilson on board the Terra Nova en route to Antarctica. I had arranged the material into twelve chapters: Early Years; Cambridge; Antarctic Preparation; Taylor in the Antarctic; Taylor's contribution to the Scott Expedition; England Again; Taylor Begins Career in Australia; The Department in Sydney; The Chicago Years; New Beginnings – University of Toronto; Retirement; Taylor's Contribution to Geography. The book also contained a list of Taylor's published works and 21 photos. It was a very special feeling to see my first book in print! I sent copies to Bill Taylor in Australia and also to the Scott Polar Research Institute in Cambridge and, of course, to my *alma mater*, the Department of Geography in Toronto.

The date of my retirement, July 1988, was fast approaching, and I had to decide what I wanted to do next. Should I stay in Windsor or leave? Should I retire from university life or try to work elsewhere? While

I was considering the alternatives, a very welcome opportunity presented itself. Bruce Mitchell, the chair of the Department of Geography at the University of Waterloo, asked me if I would like to come to Waterloo as an adjunct professor. He said that Jim Bauer, the Director of the Grand River Conservation Authority, would like to talk to me about inaugurating a water resources centre in the region. I didn't take long to decide. I knew Waterloo quite well since my sister Gwen lived there, and the challenge of starting another research centre was difficult for me to refuse. In January 1988, I was invited to Waterloo to meet the members of the Grand River Conservation Foundation, who agreed to fund the project.

My last few months in Windsor were filled with very pleasant activities. The University awarded me the title of Professor Emerita, and the City of Windsor proclaimed me "Woman of the Year." In my acceptance speech, I spoke of the few women in science, and the fact that, even in 1988, only 1% of the faculty at Windsor were female. I had only one female friend at the University – Professor Kate McCrone, an historian. I had no idea how quickly this situation would change.

It was difficult to leave Windsor, where I had lived for 38 years, where my children had been born, and where my husband had died. I had loved university life and the challenge of new students every year. I had especially enjoyed my research projects in climatology and my part in founding the Great Lakes Institute. I had renewed my interest in Arctic Canada with our Arctic Environment course. I had been at the university for 23 years, but I was not ready to retire. I enjoyed my career as a geographer and climatologist, and I looked forward to a challenging life in Waterloo. It seemed miraculous to me that as one chapter of my life ended, another interesting chapter began.

CHAPTER 7
The Water Network and UTAGA

I moved to Kitchener-Waterloo in the summer of 1988. I knew a little about its German heritage; that Kitchener had been formerly called Berlin, and that many Mennonites lived in the area. I was very happy with the town house I bought in Mennonite country near St. Jacobs, and loved seeing the horses and buggies on the roads. The University of Waterloo was a very pleasant surprise, with lots of open spaces, very unlike the urban atmosphere of the University of Windsor. I was given an office in the Department of Geography in the Faculty of Environmental Studies. The professors were all extremely kind to me; I recall especially Bruce Mitchell, Phil Howarth, Geoff Wall, Gordon Nelson, and two female professors, Trudi Bunting and Jean Andrey. After 23 years of being the only female in the department in Windsor, it was nice to have female colleagues. There were other differences from the Department of Geography at Windsor. All the professors at Waterloo had their own personal computers, while I was quite computer-illiterate. The secretary at Windsor had always done my typing. The department provided me with a computer, but I must confess that I never learned how to use it.

With the help of Bruce Mitchell and Jim Bauer, I prepared a detailed proposal for a water resources institute for the Grand River Foundation, the funding arm of the Grand River Conservation Authority. The GRCA was a very active organization, with offices located in Cambridge, not far from Waterloo. We proposed that the institute should be a multidisciplinary, multi-university research centre, based at the University of Waterloo, with the purpose of conducting research and providing advice on water management in the Grand River Basin and Ontario. We proposed that the institute should also have members from the University of Guelph, with expertise in soils and agriculture, and from Wilfrid Laurier University with expertise in business and risk management. Jim Bauer suggested the name "The Water Network" for the institute, which Bruce and I thought most appropriate. The proposal was accepted by the Grand River Foundation with funding of $50,000 for the first three years. My salary was to be $1,000 per month, and I was given permission to hire a secretary on a per-hour basis. It was agreed that the Network would have an Advisory Committee composed of 10 members; from the Foundation, government agencies, and universities. It was hoped that the Network would eventually be self-supporting with funds from research grants and conferences.

There was a good deal of interest in The Water Network from water researchers at the three universities. By December 1988, 43 scientists had requested membership; 17 from the University of Waterloo (Biology, the Centre for Groundwater Research, Civil Engineering, Earth Sciences, Environment and Resource Studies, and Geography); 21 from the University of Guelph (Agricultural Economics, Business, Crop Science, Engineering and Environmental Biology): and five from Wilfrid Laurier University (Biology, Business and Economics and Geography). All of these scientists were male. Not one female professor requested membership in The Water Network. As I had found in Windsor, female scientists did not seem interested in water!

With the help of our Advisory Committee, our first task was to decide on a research topic. The issue of climate change was becoming popular with funding agencies, and we decided that our first research effort should be a study of the impact of possible climate change on water in the Grand River Basin. The Water Network members had expertise in many aspects of water, so our subjects of research ranged from groundwater to the snow season at the local ski hill. Early in 1989, we submitted the research proposal, which included nine sub-proposals, to Environment Canada for funding. In June, we were informed that Environment Canada had granted us $42,000, and the Donner Canadian Foundation awarded us a further $70,000. The Water Network was off to a very good start.

The research was completed in the allotted time of three years, and the final report was published as a book by Waterloo's Department of Geography. It presented a detailed look at the impact of the forecast climate change on many aspects of water in the Grand River Basin. Chapter 1, written by graduate student Jamie Smith and myself, was entitled "The Present and Possible Future Climate of the Grand River Basin." (For the future climate, we used the three most popular climate change scenarios obtained from Environment Canada.) By the year 2050, the climate change scenarios forecast an increase of 4.7-5.7C° in annual temperature. The models differed in forecasting annual precipitation, from an increase of 2% to a decrease of 7%. For the Grand River region, these changes would mean an increase in annual evapotranspiration of 12-16%, an increase in water deficiency (drought) of 63-115%, and a decrease in water surplus of 15-36%. For an agricultural region like the Grand River Basin, these represented significant changes.

The chapter on the impact of potential climate change on surface water resources was written by Ed McBean (Civil Engineering, Waterloo); on groundwater by Ed Sudicky (The Centre for Groundwater Research, Waterloo); on agriculture by Gerry Hall (Geography, Wilfrid Laurier). Geoff Wall (Geography, Waterloo) wrote of the future of the local Chicopee ski hill under a warmer climate, and the effect of climate change on the Luther Marsh. The impact on water quality was the work of John Fitzgibbon (Rural Planning, Guelph); on municipal water systems and water management (John Robinson, Environment and Resource Studies, Waterloo); the policy implications for water management in the basin by Bruce Mitchell (Geography, Waterloo). The book is a very comprehensive study of the impacts of climate change on water resources in a very important part of Southern Ontario. However, at that time there was little interest in climate change among the general population, and the business members on our Advisory Committee thought it was a rather esoteric topic, and suggested that we should be doing more work on water quality.

Water quality has always been a concern in the Grand River Basin, and elsewhere, and in March 1989, The Water Network organized a "Workshop on Water Quality" at the University of Guelph, and in 1990 a Symposium on "Water Quality Issues in the Grand River Basin." Both were very well attended. Local politicians, both municipal and provincial, as well as the Grand River Conservation Authority, were very supportive of these activities on water quality. In 1991, we organized an "International Symposium on Water Pipelines and Diversions in the Great Lakes," since there was concern by both Canadian and American Great Lakes residents about diversions of water out of the lakes. This was one of our most successful conferences. We attracted a very prestigious panel of speakers from the two countries, including Tom Kierans who told us about his controversial proposal to bring James Bay water into the Great Lakes. The local media gave a good deal of publicity to our conferences.

The Water Network never submitted any further large research proposals. Preparing interdisciplinary proposals is a lot of work, and I must admit that I didn't feel equal to the task again. Our Advisory Committee liked the idea of conferences, and in 1992 we organized a conference on "Water Pollution Prevention." Another topic was "Groundwater and Wetlands," and this symposium had an interesting twist for me. As the organizer, I invited Paul Martin (at the time he was the Liberal environment critic in the House of Commons) to be the guest speaker. I had known Paul for many years, as a neighbour in Windsor, and the son of our Windsor M.P., Paul Martin Sr. Of course Paul was well-known to everyone in Windsor, but I hadn't realized that he wasn't well-known in K.W. He gave a very good speech, and during the question period, one woman asked him "Which political party are you with?" Little did we know that Paul would become the Prime Minister of Canada in 2003! Our next symposium focussed on "Groundwater Protection." The emphasis on groundwater was understandable since the University of Waterloo had a well-known Centre for Groundwater Research, and groundwater is the major source of water in the K.W. area. A most successful conference on "Water and First Nations" was held in 1995 at the Woodland Cultural Centre in Brantford, co-sponsored by the Cayuga Nation of First Nations. This was the first time that aboriginal scientists and tribal leaders were involved in any of our conferences. In 1996, we returned to the issue of water quantity with a conference on "Water Quantity Management in Ontario," co-hosted by the Ontario Ministry of Natural Resources and the Canadian Water Resources Association.

In 1993, I realized that I had become a senior academic when I received a letter from the President of Ryerson Polytechnic Institute (now Ryerson University) stating that the Institute would like to give me a Ryerson Fellowship, their highest honour. Of course I accepted, and went to Toronto for the occasion. Nick Siller, a geography graduate from the University of Windsor and a professor at Ryerson, read the citation. I have always loved convocations, and being honoured at a convocation was a new and exciting experience for me.

Also, during the 1990s, with no teaching duties at Waterloo, I had more time to travel. I went frequently to Hawaii, because I loved the Islands, and also to check with my co-authors on our book on the climate of Hawaii. I was invited to a water conference in Helsinki, Finland, my first visit to a Scandinavian country. It seemed very much like Canada to me. I recall that all the participants spoke English, and that we were invited to private homes for typical Finnish food. After the conference, I took a ferry to Denmark and bought a Eurail Pass for a trip to Austria. I had never been to Vienna and I wanted to see that historic city and go to the opera. I also managed to see a performance by the famous Lipizzaner stallions. I re-discovered the charm of the Algarve in Portugal, spending a month there in the winter of 1992 and again in 1995. It was lovely to escape the Canadian winters in February and see the almond trees in bloom. I took a tour to Seville in Spain and also that famous bastion of the British Empire, Gibraltar. It was exciting to think that Africa was so close, so I also managed a day trip to Tangier in Morocco.

I maintained my association with the International Hydrological Programme and in 1993 I was invited to Thailand to an international water conference to speak about our work on the impact of climate change on the Great Lakes. The conference was held in Bangkok in a very elegant setting, and the delegates were welcomed by a princess of the royal family of Thailand. My main memories of Bangkok were the crowds, the exotic food, and the many canals and rivers. The conference organizers had arranged a post-conference tour to the city of Chiang Mai in northern Thailand. There I had the unusual experiences of riding on an elephant – rather scary – and having a rafting trip on one of the large rivers. We heard later that on one such trip, the raft was hijacked by bandits who relieved the tourists of all their money and jewellery. After the conference, I stopped for a few days in Hong Kong. What a fabulous setting for a city. I stayed at the beautiful Four Seasons Hotel in Kowloon, and took the ferry to Hong Kong Island and the funicular railway to the top of the mountain.

About this time, because of my work on climate change, I was invited to be a member of the Environmental Adaptation Research Group (EARG) of Environment Canada, by its director Roger Street. Although based in the Environment Canada offices in Downsview, EARG had research groups at the University of Toronto, the University of British Columbia, and the University of Waterloo. The objectives of these groups were to investigate the impacts of, and adaptation to, possible climate change. In 1995, Ian Burton, a geographer with EARG, organized a trip to Beijing, China, to meet with Chinese climate change scientists, and I was invited to be a participant. Beijing looked very different to me in 1995 from the city I had seen in 1987. This time our accommodation was in a very modern hotel and there were many foreign tourists. I noticed many more cars on the highways, but the explosion of high-rise hotels had not yet occurred. As on my previous visit, we were taken to the Great Wall, the Ming Tombs and the Forbidden City. Our discussions with the Chinese scientists were about climate change, but I got the impression that the topic was not one of great concern for them.

I never tire of visiting Europe. In 1997, I had an interesting trip to Greece, to Athens and Delphi again, as Bob and I had done in 1967, but this time also to the island of Crete. I had always wanted to see the ruins at Knossos and they were awe-inspiring. It was March, a low-tourist season, so the few of us from our hotel had the ruins to ourselves. I have a reproduction of one of the frescos in my apartment still. I also enjoyed winter vacations in the Caribbean, discovering the

Mayan Riviera area of Mexico, Cuba and the Dominican Republic. I have become accustomed to travelling alone.

Although most of my time in Waterloo was spent on Water Network business, I never forgot my interest in Arctic Canada, and I found other geographers at who were interested in the Arctic. Phil Howarth and Paul Kay and I decided to revive The Arctic Environment course, choosing Igloolik as the location because of its beautiful and functional research centre. We wrote to John MacDonald, the director of the centre and were given permission to hold our course there in July 1993. Eighteen students signed up for the course, although we were disappointed that none were northerners. It was a great feeling to be flying north again. There were many changes. Frobisher Bay was now Iqaluit, and the future Nunavut was in the planning stages. Igloolik looked the same – no movie makers yet! John MacDonald was very helpful in arranging a house for us to live, and cook in. Our program was different from the earlier years since we didn't have Paul Hebert to do the biology, but we did a good job on the climate, geomorphology and hydrology of that interesting island. For most of the students, just being in the Arctic in the land of the midnight sun, was an unforgettable experience. We spent a few days at the end of the course in Iqaluit staying, of course, at Ukkivik. It was a nostalgic experience for me, since I think I knew that it would be my last visit to Arctic Canada. What a fascinating part of Canada, and how lucky I have been to have seen so much of it!

In 1990 I received a letter from the (then) Minister of National Defence David Collenette, inviting me to serve on an Environmental Advisory Committee of the Department of National Defence. The role of the committee was to review the Department's environmental policies and procedures. I knew nothing about Canada's DND, but I thought it would be interesting to learn. Our committee met in the Defence headquarters in Ottawa. The 10 members from across Canada were biologists, engineers, geographers and one retired general. I recall that there were lots of briefings from DND personnel about environmental procedures at various locations across Canada. More interesting were our visits to several Canadian Forces Bases. Suffield in Alberta and Halifax stand out in my memory; the former because of the wild horses on the property, and Halifax since we had a tour of a naval destroyer. The committee raised the question of visiting one of the DEW Line stations in the Arctic, but this never happened. (At the time northern residents were becoming concerned about the pollution at the abandoned DEW Line stations.) We submitted a report to the Minister after three years, and in 1994 the committee was reduced to five members (luckily I was one), and in 1996 it was terminated. I never found out what prompted the government to investigate DND's environmental record, nor the reason for the discontinuation of the committee. However, the clean-up of the DEW Line stations is taking place, so perhaps we did some good.

Finally, in 1993, after six years in the writing, the book on the climate of Hawaii was published by the University of Hawaii Press with the title *Prevailing Trade Winds*. The authors were the original six who had agreed to contribute when we first talked about the book in 1987: Paul Ekern, Tom Giambelluca, Dennis Nullet, Saul Price, Tom Schroeder and myself. We agreed with the Press that the title was appropriate given that the feature that best identifies the Hawaiian climate is the prevailing wind, which provides the natural air-conditioning for the Islands. My main contributions to the book, in addition to acting as editor, were the sections on temperature and rainfall, the water balance and climate classification.

The authors of 'Prevailing Trade Winds' - left to right: Thomas Schroeder, Paul Ekern, me, Tom Giambelluca, Dennis Nullet (absent Saul Price)

I explained that, because of the location of the Islands in the middle of the Pacific Ocean, temperatures vary little from winter to summer. At the Honolulu International Airport at sea level, the average maximum temperature in August, the warmest month, is 31.5°C and the average minimum is 23.4°C. During the coldest month, January, the maximum is 26.7°C and the minimum 18.6°C, a difference of only 4.5C° in both cases. Of course, higher elevations have cooler temperatures. At the observing station at 3,400 metres on Mauna Loa, the average temperature is only 6.7°C. Precipitation varies greatly in the Islands. In Honolulu, the average rainfall is 560 mm while a few miles inland, at the head of Manoa Valley, the average is 4,000 mm. Mount Waialeale in Kauai has an average annual rainfall of 11,430 mm, one of the wettest places on earth. The Islands have climates varying from tundra at the tops of the high mountains on the Big Island, to tropical rain forest on the windward sides of the islands, to desert conditions on the leeward coasts. It is understandable that the popular tourist areas in the islands are on the dry leeward coasts.

Tom Schroeder described the climate controls, Dennis Nullet the radiation and energy balances and past climatic changes, and Tom Giambelluca the water balance. Paul Ekern wrote about climate and agriculture, especially the culture of sugar cane and pineapples. Saul Price wrote about climate and human activity; and Hawaii as a place to visit, live and work. He described the sites on the Big Island, near the summits of Mauna Loa and Mauna Kea, where the atmosphere is very clear, making them ideal for research on climate change and astronomy. The many maps and diagrams in the book were the work of Ev Wingert of the Department of Geography. Altogether it is a very attractive book. In the preface it is stated, "We hope we make understandable the reasons for the loveliness of the climate of Hawaii, truly the climate of Paradise."

I had moved to Waterloo in 1988, and had worked hard to establish The Water Network. However, in 1995, it became obvious to me that the Network had financial troubles. The grant from the Grand River Foundation had run out, and the income from our conferences did not cover expenses. Again, Jim Bauer had a solution. He told me that the Canadian Water Resources Association needed an editor for its quarterly journal, the *Canadian Water Resources Journal*, and they would pay $400 a month stipend. He suggested that I should apply for the job, since I could combine it with my Water Network duties, and continue with the conferences. I became the editor of the *Canadian Water Resources Journal,* a job I enjoyed for the next eight years. I had never been an editor before, but I found it very interesting. Papers submitted for publication were sent to me, and I sent each one to two reviewers. Since I had been in the water business for some time, I had no problem finding qualified reviewers. The reviewers either refused the paper or accepted it, usually with modifications. If there was disagreement, I sent the paper to a third reviewer. Usually modifications were suggested, and these I sent to the author. When I received the final paper, I edited it for spelling and grammar. My secretary did the word processing and the final paper in diskette form was sent to the publisher. Amazingly I still hadn't learned to use a computer!

As a climatologist, as well as the director of The Water Network, I saw the need for a book on the climate of the Grand River Basin. I found that there were 13 weather stations in the 7,000 sq. km. area, and quite a range of climate types, from cool and wet in the north at Monticello to warmer and drier at Dunnville on the Lake Erie shore. The book was finished in 1998 and published by the Grand River Foundation with the title *The Grand Climate: Weather and Water in the Grand River Basin.* On the back cover it was stated, "The Grand Climate presents the facts of climate and weather in easily understood language with many tables and illustrations. Marie Sanderson answers your questions about the Grand climate, but didn't know who to ask."

Also in the mid-1990s, my friend and former student, David Phillips, Senior Climatologist at Environment Canada, suggested that I do a monograph on the climate of the twin cities of Kitchener-Waterloo, as one of Environment Canada's series on the climates of Canadian cities. I enjoyed doing the research for this book. I found that there were seven weather stations in and around the urban area, some with records dating from 1915. I wrote about "Who are the weather observers?" "The highs, the lows, and the means of temperature" "When and how much does it rain?" and "Has there been, will there be, climate change?" The Department of Geography at the University of Waterloo published the book in 1996, with the title *Weather and Climate in Kitchener-Waterloo, Ontario.*

While in Waterloo, I continued to attend the annual meetings of the

Canadian Association of Geographers as well as those of the Association of American Geographers. It was a good chance to renew acquaintances with my Canadian and American geography friends. I was invited to join the Climatology Specialty Group of the AAG. I looked forward to seeing my friend Russ Mather from Delaware at these meetings. In the early 1990s, Russ and I decided that we should collaborate on a biography of our friend and mentor, Warren Thornthwaite. It was a labour of love for both of us. We sent the book to the University of Oklahoma Press (Thornthwaite had been a professor of geography at that university), and were pleased to have it accepted. It was published in 1996 with the title *The Genius of C. Warren Thornthwaite: Climatologist-Geographer*. In our book, Russ and I concluded, "Thornthwaite changed the course of climatology in 20th century North America by stressing that climatology is a rigorous discipline defined by physical laws, not the computing of average values of temperature and precipitation," as it had previously been defined. We also wrote, "He was the founder of the field of applied climatology, the solving of practical problems of irrigation scheduling, and crop harvesting, as he had shown so successfully at Seabrook Farms. His water budget model has been proven to be useful to scores of scientists within and outside the realm of climatology." We concluded, "He possessed that spark of genius, that ability to postulate new ideas and solve complex problems that is rarely encountered."

In 1998, I received a very exciting letter from the president of the University of Waterloo, stating that the University would like to give me an Honorary Doctorate in Environmental Studies. I was also asked to give the convocation address. I have always loved the pomp and circumstance of convocations, and I think nothing can be compared to the feeling I experienced when the chancellor put the University of Waterloo hood on my shoulders! In my address to the graduands, I spoke about women in science, Mary Somerville in particular, and my own experience as a woman in academic geography in Canada. That day was a wonderful climax to my ten years at Waterloo!

I felt that it was time to leave Waterloo. I had enjoyed my colleagues in Geography very much, I had had several books published, and had helped to establish an interdisciplinary water research institute. I decided in the summer of 1998 to move to Toronto where my two sons lived. Also, Roger Street, the director of the research group now called AIRG (Adaptation and Impacts Research Group) suggested that I could have a desk and computer in the AIRG office in the Institute for Environmental Studies at the University of Toronto. This association sounded good to me and I was happy to accept. I also had a job to keep me busy, since I was still the editor of the *Canadian Water Resources Journal*, and I could do that at the University of Toronto as easily as at Waterloo. Roger decided that I must have a computer, although I told him that I didn't know how to use one. He organized an instructor for me and I recall our first meeting. I said, "Please start at the beginning and write down the instructions." I kept those instructions for some time. They began, "Push button on the box on the floor to turn the computer on." So, finally, I entered the computer age.

It was nostalgic to be back at UofT after so many years. I made contact with the Department of Geography, situated on the fifth floor of Sidney Smith Hall. My old friend Don Kerr invited me to become a member of the Historical Committee of UTAGA (University of Toronto Association of Geography Alumni). Dick Baine and Bob Putnam were also at the first meeting I attended. Don suggested that, since I had written a biography of Taylor, the first chair of Geography at Toronto, a biography of Donald Putnam, the second professor hired, should be the next project of the historical committee. Dr Putnam had played a very important role in my life, as these pages have shown, and I was very happy to volunteer to work on his biography, with Bob Putnam as co-author. I immediately went to the University Archives at the Fisher Library of the University of Toronto to look at the Putnam material. There were 12 series, from "Diaries" to "Teaching Notes" to "Articles and Books," presenting a history of Putnam's life from his early days in Nova Scotia, to the Ontario Research Foundation, to the University of Toronto, to his final days at Erindale.

The book, *Down to Earth: A Biography of Geographer Donald Fulton Putnam*, was published in 2000 as a millenium project of the Department of Geography. For the cover, we decided to use a reproduction of part of the map (in full colour) from the 1984 edition of Chapman and Putnam's *The Physiography of Southern Ontario.* Our book contained eight chapters; The Early Years; Putnam, Chapman and the Ontario Research Foundation; Geography at the University of Toronto: the Taylor Years; The Joint Headship; Putnam at the Helm; Putnam and High School

Geography; The Erindale Years; and The Legacy. It was another labour of love on my part for a professor who had been a good friend to me. In the concluding chapter, we stated that, "Without doubt, Putnam's greatest contribution to geography, and indeed to earth sciences in Canada, was his work with Lyman Chapman on the landforms of Southern Ontario, which has had three editions, and is a classic to this day."

The Department of Geography at UofT, with chair Joe Desloges, organized a book launch in June 2000 at Victoria College, and more than 100 former students and friends of "Putty" attended, an indication of his popularity as a teacher and advisor. We had included in the book many comments about him from his former students. Many mentioned that he had inspired in them a love of landscape and landforms, as well as recalling his absentmindedness and falling asleep during his own lectures. He would have liked the statement on the back cover: "Donald Putnam profoundly influenced a generation of geographers, and played a major role in establishing geography as an academic subject in the high schools of Ontario." He would also have liked the title of the book "Down to Earth" which certainly described his outlook on life.

I felt very much like a senior academic in 1999, when I received a letter from the president of the University of Windsor, stating that they would like to honour me with an honorary degree of Doctor of Philosophy at the June convocation. I was also invited to give the convocation address. My friend from my Windsor teaching days, historian Kathleen McCrone, read the citation. I rightly sensed that the honour was because of my work with the Great Lakes Institute, so that was the subject of my address. It was gratifying to know that the GLI has prospered, with its new title "Institute for Great Lakes and Environmental Research." It was nostalgic to be in Windsor again, and to see old friends and university colleagues. In 2000, I received another honorary degree, this time from the University of Lethbridge in Alberta. I had never been to Lethbridge, and thoroughly enjoyed being shown around the area and wined and dined by Ian MacLachlan and Tom Johnston of the Department of Geography. My daughter daughter Susan, son-in-law Tom and their family from Calgary were also honoured guests. I have vivid memories of the day of convocation. I caught a cold and completely lost my voice! I love to talk, so it was very annoying not to be able to speak on that special day. Luckily I had not been asked to give the convocation address.

It was a great honour to receive an honorary degree
from the University of Windsor in 1999

As a true geographer, I continued to enjoy travelling. In 1999, I
spent three wonderful weeks in Hawaii, first at the AAG conference in
Honolulu, and then in Maui with my daughter Susan, son-in-law Tom
and their family. At the end of that year, I decided to welcome the new
millennium in Malta, and spent two weeks on that interesting island
at the crossroads of the Mediterranean. It has 3,000 years of history,
and was very important during the Crusades. I especially remember
the capital, Valetta, and the museums commemorating the special role
that Malta played during the Second World War. Its excellent harbour
was important for allied shipping, and many people had starved when
the island was blockaded by the Germans. I also learned that St. Paul
had spent a winter in Malta when he was being taken as a prisoner to
Rome.

In 2001, I travelled to Bali in Indonesia, a part of the world I had
never visited. It was a long flight, with an overnight stop in Tokyo. I
had not known that most people in Bali were Hindu, so the island
brought back memories of India. The hotel was lovely, and I found the
Balinese people most attractive and the music quite exotic. I went on a

tour into the mountains, visited a local village, and saw lots of temples. The next year, I spent two weeks in the winter in Morocco, in Agadir on the Atlantic coast. This was my first time in a Moslem country. The first unusual thing was that my hotel was built on a hill overlooking the ocean, with the lobby at the top and the rooms at various levels descending to a promenade along the ocean. The tourists were mostly Moroccan and German. I was seated at a table with some very nice German people, and with their good English and my poor German, we managed quite pleasant conversations. I took a tour into the interior, and was surprised to see snow on the Atlas Mountains, and a rather unusual sight, goats that climbed trees.

At the UofT, while I kept quite busy with my editorial work, I felt that I needed another larger project, and decided that I should update the monograph on the climate of southern Ontario, written originally by Chapman and Putnam in 1938, and revised by Chapman, Brown and McKay in 1968. The Chapman *et al.* publication was in Imperial units. There were now 30 more years of data, and Canada had become metric. This job was rather nostalgic since one of my first publications, while at the Ontario Research Foundation in 1950, had been *Moisture Relationships in Southern Ontario*. Thus, I was very familiar with the locations of the climate stations in southern Ontario, and chose 57 manned stations to represent the various climatic regions in Southern Ontario. I used the 1971-2000 averages published by Environment Canada for the period of record. In the Introduction I stated "This book is written for Ontario residents, who, like all Canadians, love to talk about weather and climate. Weather is rarely monotonous in southern Ontario. Consider its location in the pathway of the majority of storms that track across North America, and in the convergence zone between cool dry continental air and warm moist ocean air. Add the influence of the Great Lakes and the diversity of city and country landscapes, and the result is a climatic region where weather is often restless, mostly unpredictable and always interesting."

The largest chapters, of course, dealt with temperature and precipitation, and included maps of annual and seasonal as well as extreme values. There were chapters on urban climates, climate information for farmers and gardeners, climate variability and the possible future climate of the region. I intended the book to be a source book on the current climate of the region, where the reader could find the actual data. An added feature of the book was a chapter on "Weather Disasters" kindly written by David Phillips. David wrote that the worst non-maritime weather disaster in Canada was the heat wave of 1936 (one I remembered personally). The book was published by the Department of Geography, University of Waterloo in 2004 with the title *Weather and Climate in Southern Ontario.*

I usually travel alone, but in 2003 I decided to take my two teenaged granddaughters to the Algarve in Portugal. It was their first trip to Europe, so it was interesting to see some of my favourite places through their young eyes. We went to Cape St. Vincent to see the "western end of Europe," and the girls listened wide-eyed when the guide said, "On a clear day here, you can see America." We visited Seville in Spain, and the girls loved the cathedral and the tomb of Christopher Columbus. They were the only young people in our hotel, so they were the centre of attention. In 2004, I was again in Hawaii with son Jimmy, daughter-in-law Dianne and their family.

In 2006, my granddaughter was in school in Italy so I visited her in historic Lanciano and saw again the incredible sights of Rome. It had been many years since I had been to Rome, and the number of tourists had increased unbelievably. The wait to enter the Vatican was an hour long, and the crowds around the Trevi Fountain were so large it was almost impossible to throw a coin in the fountain. But I saw a few places I hadn't visited before, the Borghese Gardens and the very lovely Doria Pamphili private museum.

I chose Lanzarote in the Canary Islands for a holiday in 2007. It is a Spanish island off the coast of Morocco, a most unusual island with black lava landscape reminding me of parts of Hawaii. The Gran Melia Volcan was a beautiful hotel and the weather was warm and it never rained – a perfect holiday. In 2008, I went to Madeira, a Portuguese island to the north of the Canary Islands. It is quite different from Lanzarote, with hardly a square metre of level ground. Most of the tourists in my hotel were German. Although there has been a huge increase in the number of tourists, one thing seems not to have changed. Very few women travel alone. Usually, I am the only woman sitting alone in the hotel dining room. This is a mystery to me since I have never had a bad experience, and I will continue to travel alone as long as I am able.

As a climatologist for some 60 years, I have often been asked about the widespread concern about global warming, and the statements that the warming is caused by human-induced increases in atmospheric CO_2. I have read the reports of the IPCC (Intergovernmental Panel on Climate Change), the most recent of which was published in 2007. The projections of future climate are based on computer models which have been greatly criticized by world scientists. There are a great number of uncertainties in the input data, especially with regard to cloudiness, particulate matter and especially water vapour. (How many people know that water vapour is the most important greenhouse gas?) With so many uncertainties in the input, the model output of future temperatures is very suspect. The projections of future precipitation amounts are even more questionable, as even the modellers themselves have stated. Many reputable world scientists are "sceptics" about CO_2-induced global warming. Unfortunately, their views don't receive the publicity given to the "gloom and doom" reports.

I remember that only a few decades ago there was widespread concern about an imminent ice age. Anyone who has studied geology knows that the climate is always changing; that for most of the earth's history, the climate has been warmer than at present; and that only 12,000 years ago, most of Canada was covered by glaciers. Usually not mentioned in the climate change literature is the fact that our record of world temperatures in very short. As I pointed out earlier in this book, the systematic gathering of air temperature data dates only from the middle of the 19th century, a very short period in the lifetime of the earth.

To return to my life story, I feel that I have come full circle – from the University of Toronto in the 1940s, to the University of Maryland, the University of Michigan, the University of Windsor, the University of Waterloo, and in 1998, back to the University of Toronto. I am happy to be back in Toronto. It is interesting to be involved with UTAGA and its History Committee. After we produced the book about Donald Putnam, John Warkentin of the History Committee wrote an excellent biography of the third member of the department, George Tatham. It was entitled *The Art of Geography: The Life and Teaching of George*

Tatham. In 2004, for the 100th anniversary meeting of the AAG in Philadelphia, we produced a poster of the life of Griffith Taylor. I took the poster to the meeting and was very impressed with the number of delegates who had met or had some connection with Taylor. The next year, we produced a poster of the history of the department at UofT for the CAG meeting at the University of Western Ontario in London. These two posters are now on display in the department. In 2006, we helped the department to procure a vintage photograph of Taylor in his sledging gear taken by Herbert Ponting in the Antarctic in 1911. I think Grif would be pleased to know that UofT geography students in the 21st century will gaze on this photo of the founder of the department.

EPILOGUE

I look back on my life as a geographer-climatologist with much pleasure. I was indeed blessed with parents who were decades ahead of their time in believing that a daughter should receive a postgraduate as well as an undergraduate university education. I was similarly blessed with an understanding husband who, unlike most of his contemporaries, believed that a wife should have her own career. I was indeed lucky that Griffith Taylor was my mentor at the University of Toronto and that he suggested geography as my field of study. It was my great good fortune to study with the renowned climatologist C.W. Thornthwaite at the University of Maryland and become a climatologist. I have had the privilege of being a professor of geography at the University of Windsor for 23 years, and for a short time at the University of Hawaii. After retirement, I have had happy associations with the University of Waterloo and the University of Toronto. I have enjoyed the students, and I have especially enjoyed the research in climatology, from measuring potential evapotranspiration to mapping the climates of Canada, and from precipitation chemistry to explaining the causes of fluctuating Great Lakes levels. Of special importance to me was the founding of the Great Lakes Institute at the University of Windsor, and The Water Network at Waterloo. My time in Arctic Canada, doing research or with the Arctic Environment courses, was something never to be forgotten. An added bonus during my career has been meeting geographers and climatologists from around the world.

I have written a great deal about my travels outside North America. I think all geographers love to travel and see for themselves what this world looks like. There are still a few places I would like to visit, although at age 87, I wonder how many more travelling years I have left. People often ask me "What is your favourite place?" Inverhuron, on beautiful Lake Huron, is my favourite place in the world. It is the place to which I return, no matter where I happen to be living. Hawaii and Arctic Canada, so different, yet so interesting, are tied for second place in my affection.

The scientific and academic world for women today is very different from the world I knew. At the University of Windsor in the late 1960s there were only two female professors outside the Faculty of Nursing. When I retired in 1988, female professors still made up only 1% of the University of Windsor faculty. My academic world was exclusively a male world, and my mentors have all been male. The discipline of geography has changed greatly during my lifetime. The first department of geography in Canada was established at the University of Toronto only in 1935. In 2008 the Canadian Association of Geographers Directory listed 45 universities in Canada with geography departments. My story as a student and professor of geography during the almost-60-year period 1940 to 1998 may serve as a microcosm of the discipline during those years.

During my career there have been some interesting highlights. In 1949 I conducted the first climate experiment in Canada's Arctic. In 1965 I was the first female professor of geography in Canada. I was one of the organizers of the first university credit course in the Arctic, and the founding director of the University of Windsor's Great Lakes Institute. I was the first female president of the Canadian Association of Geographers. Four Canadian universities have honoured me. I have had a very good life as a geographer and climatologist.

PUBLISHED BOOKS

1980   *The Climate of the Essex Region, Canada's Southland*, Department of Geography, University of Windsor, 101 pp.

1988   *Griffith Taylor: Antarctic Scientist and Pioneer Geographer*, Carleton University Press, 300 pp.

1990   *UNESCO Sourcebook in Climatology for Hydrologists and Water Resource Engineers*, UNESCO Press, Paris, 109 pp.

1993   *Letters From a Soldier* (co-author, R.M. Sanderson), Escart Press, University of Waterloo, 213 pp.

1993   *The Impact of Climate Change on Water in the Grand River Basin* (editor), Department of Geography Publication Series No. 40, University of Waterloo, 223 pp.

1993   *Prevailing Trade Winds: Weather and Climate in Hawai'i* (editor), University of Hawaii Press, Honolulu, Hawaii, 126 pp.

1996   *The Genius of C. Warren Thornthwaite: Climatologist – Geographer* (with J.R. Mather), University of Oklahoma Press, 225 pp.

1996   *Weather and Climate in Kitchener-Waterloo, Ontario*, Department of Geography Publication Series No. 46, University of Waterloo, 110 pp.

1998   *The Grand Climate: Weather and Water in the Grand River Basin*, The Grand River Foundation, 120 pp.

2000   *Down to Earth: A Biography of Donald Fulton Putnam* (with Robert Putnam), University of Toronto, Department of Geography, 144 pp.

2004   *Weather and Climate in Southern Ontario*, Department of Geography Publication Series No. 58, University of Waterloo, 126 pp.

JOURNAL ARTICLES

1948   "The climates of Canada according to the new Thornthwaite classification" *Canadian Journal of Plant Science*, 28, 501-517.

1948   "Drought in the Canadian Northwest" *Geographical Review*, 38, 289-299.

1948   "An experiment to measure potential evapotranspiration" *Canadian Journal of Research*, Section C, 26, 445-454.

1950   "Moisture relationships in Southern Ontario" *Canadian Journal of Plant Science*, 30, 235-255.

1950   "Measuring potential evapotranspiration at Norman Wells, 1949" *Geographical Review*, 50 (4), 636-645.

1950   "Three years of evapotranspiration at Toronto" *Canadian Journal of Research*, Section C, 28, 482-492.

1950   "Is Canada's Northwest subhumid?" *Canadian Geographical Journal*, 41 (3), 142-146.

1950   "Some Canadian developments in agricultural meteorology and climatology" *Weather*, 5 (11), 381-412.

1954   "Observations of potential evapotranspiration at Windsor, Ontario" John Hopkins University Lab. of Climatology, *Publications in Climatology*, 7, 91-93.

1971   "Variability of annual runoff in the Lake Ontario basin" *Water Resources Research*, 7, 554-565.

1972   "Climatology at the International Geographical Congress, Montreal, 1972" *McGill Climatological Bulletin*, October, 23-42.

1972   "The variability of some terrestrial water balance parameters in the Lake Ontario basin" C.W. Thornthwaite Associates, Lab. of Climatology, *Publications in Climatology*, 25 (2), 39-45.

1973   "Three aspects of the urban climate of Detroit-Windsor" *Journal of Applied Meteorology*, 12 (4), 629-638.

1974   "Mary Somerville – her work in physical geography" *Geographical Review*, 64 (3), 410-420.

1974   "A preliminary radiation climatology of Windsor, Ontario" *McGill Climatological Bulletin*, October, 1-12.

1975   "A comparison of Canadian and United States standard methods of measuring precipitation" *Journal of Applied Meteorology*, 14 (6), 1197-1199.

1976   "Monthly precipitation probability maps for the growing season in southern Ontario" *Canadian Journal of Plant Science*, 56, 639-645.

1976   "A climatologist in the Soviet Union" *McGill Climatological Bulletin*, October, 17-24.

1978   "The effect of Metropolitan Detroit-Windsor on precipitation" (with R. Gorski) *Journal of Applied Meteorology*, 17 (4), 423-427.

1979   "Surface loadings from pollutants in precipitation in Southern Ontario: some climatic and statistical aspects" (with P.D. LaValle) *Journal Great Lakes Research*, 5 (1), 52-60.

1979   "Potential evapotranspiration and water deficit in Bangladesh using Garnier's modification of the Thornthwaite water balance" (with R. Ahmed) *McGill Climatological Bulletin*, 2, 13-24.

1979   "Pre-monsoon rainfall and its variability in Bangladesh: a trend surface analysis" (with R. Ahmed) *Hydrological Sciences Bulletin*, 24 (3), 277-287.

1982   "Climatology in Canada: Impressions over three decades" *Climatological Bulletin*, 31, April, 1-6.

1982   "Griffith Taylor: a geographer to remember" *The Canadian Geographer*, 26 (4), 293-299.

1983   "Heating degree-day research in Alberta-residents conserve natural gas" *Professional Geographer*, 35 (4), 437-440.

1983   "Summer at Ukkivik" *The Beaver*, Hudson's Bay Company, Spring, 30-35.

1985   "Surface loading of lead and cadmium from precipitation in

Essex County" (with D. Marchand and P. MacQuarrie) *Journal Great Lakes Research* 11 (3), 305-312.

1985   "Climates of Canada" *The Canadian Encyclopedia*, Hurtig Publishers, 353-354.

1985   "St. Clair River" *The Canadian Encylopedia*, Hurtig Publishers, 1618.

1985   "Lake St. Clair" *The Canadian Encyclopedia*, Hurtig Publishers, 1618.

1985   "Taylor, Thomas Griffith" *The Canadian Encyclopedia*, Hurtig Publishers, 1788.

1987   "Implications of climatic change for navigation and power generation in the Great Lakes" *Climate Change Digest CCD 87-03*, Atmospheric Environment Service, Environment Canada.

1986   "The blob" *The Canadian Geographer*, 30 (4), 315.

1987   "The geographer as director of a multi-disciplinary institute" *The Operational Geographer*, 12, 40.

1988   "Climatic change and Great Lakes levels: the impact on shipping" (with D. Marchand, D. Howe and C. Alpaugh) *Climatic Change*, 12, 107-133.

1989   "Concentrations of two organic contaminants in precipitation, soils and plants in the Essex Region of southern Ontario" (with M. Weis) *Atmospheric Pollution*, 59, 41-54.

1989   "Water levels in the Great Lakes – past, present, future" *Ontario Geography*, 33, 1-21.

1992   "Climate change and water in the Great Lakes Basin in Ontario" Canadian Water Resources Association Newsletter, *Water News*, 11 (2), 4.

1992   "Why university-based water institutes?" *Canadian Water Resources Journal*, 17 (4), 351-356.

1993   "Climate change and water in the Great Lakes Basin" *Canadian Water Resources Journal*, 18 (4), 417-424.

1995   "Groundwater contamination in the Kitchener-Waterloo area, Ontario" (with P. Karrow, J. Greenhouse, G. Poloschi, G. Schneider, G. Mulamoottil, C. Mason, E. McBean, P.

Fitzpatrick, B. Mitchell, D. Shrubsole and E. Child) *Canadian Water Resources Journal*, 20 (3), 145-160.

1996 Obituary. "Chun-fen Lee 1914-1996" (with D. Kerr and K.C. Tan) *The Canadian Geographer*, 40 (2), 181.

1999 "The classification of climates from Pythagoras to Köppen" *Bulletin, American Meteorological Society*, 80 (4) 669-673.